SUSAN BEECH

A Petal Unfolds

HOW TO MAKE PAPER FLOWERS

PAVILION

For Jon and Grayson

First published in the United Kingdom in 2022 by
Pavilion
43 Great Ormond Street
London
WC1N 3HZ

ISBN 978-1-911663-72-0

A CIP catalogue record for this book is available
from the British Library.

10 9 8 7 6 5 4 3 2 1

Reproduction by Rival Colour Ltd., UK
Printed and bound by Toppan Leefung
Printing Ltd, China
www.pavilionbooks.com

Photographer: Ola Smit
Props stylist: Milly Bruce
Commissioning editor: Sophie Allen
Design manager: Alice Kennedy-Owen

Contents

Flowers

Projects

Introduction

My love of nature goes back to my childhood, which was spent growing up on a farm in Staffordshire. I developed a deep closeness to the natural world. Looking back, the colours, the beauty and the romanticism of the countryside have never left me. I moved away to go to the University of Brighton to do a degree in Fine Art Printmaking, but my work was heavily influenced by the grandness of nature and where I had come from.

I started working with paper in 2013, after previously making a lot of digital work. I felt a real need to go back to making with my hands again. As I spent more and more time working with crepe paper in particular, and discovering what could be done with it, the possibilities seemed endless. It still feels magical to be able to make something so realistic from such simple materials as crepe paper, glue and wire. I hope that through this book you will discover the same sense of wonder and excitement in the making and the materials too.

As a rule, I love to create flowers that are realistic, although it isn't always the most important thing for me. I love there to be some whimsy that also captures the essence and gestures of the flower. When you go on to make your own flowers, over time you will develop your own style of working with paper, as well as start to understand what is most important to you when you're making them.

This book takes you through everything, from taking your first steps with how to cut and shape crepe paper, through to putting together a multitude of hydrangea florets and creating an arrangement and bouquet. Once you learn the standard techniques of flower making, you can go on to make your own templates and your own flowers in your own way.

The flower tutorials within this book have been specially put together to cover a good range of techniques: from the simple to the more complex. Each flower also has qualities that have really resonated with me, and often with the people who have attended my workshops. If you are new to making flowers then I would recommend starting with easier flowers such as anemone, narcissus, poppy and crocus. If you are looking for more challenging flowers I would suggest hydrangea, hollyhock and dahlia.

As with any craft, it does take time and patience at first to learn the techniques, so don't be too hard on yourself when you're starting out. Have fun and experiment. You will be well on your way once some of the basic techniques have been mastered. I hope you enjoy the projects within the book and that flower making brings you many moments of happiness and beautiful creations.

How to use this book

We'll get started in the following sections with guiding you through the materials that we use and why we use them, along with the key techniques for making the flowers that follow. I would recommend that you spend some time familiarising yourself with these before getting started on your making. You could even practise some of the techniques and experiment with some of the materials.

Included in the book are 25 flower projects to make with step-by-step instructions. Measurements are given throughout in width x height. Materials required for each individual flower are listed at the beginning of each project. With the crepe papers and some of the other materials, manufacturers' reference numbers have been given where possible to clarify exactly which colours have been used.

Do feel free to adapt the tutorials wherever you feel the need to. I use the paper and materials that I feel work best and that will get the results that are shown in the photographs. However, if you would prefer to use an alternative that you have more easily to hand then please do try it.

I hope you find that this book gives you a thorough knowledge in making paper flowers and that you go on to make wonderful projects.

Anatomy of a flower & leaf

To help identify the different parts of the flower and leaves, this shows some of the terms that you may come across when working on the flower projects. I'm not a botanist, but these are the terms that I frequently use.

Leaflets

Leaf sprig

Floret

Petals

Calyx

Stamen

Carpel Centre

Materials and tools

Crepe paper

I use crepe paper to make all my flowers because unlike traditional papers, such as card, it has stretch so it can easily be made into a shape. It also has a lovely organic quality that lends itself really well to making paper flowers. Quality papers are different to the crepe you might have encountered before that is often thin and difficult to do anything with – they're much stronger. When I first started making flowers it was really difficult to get hold of but now there are a lot more papers and colours available.

When making a flower for the first time I'll often choose which papers to use by looking closely at the real flower and observing the texture, shape and the colour. I'll then trial the flower in the paper I feel is most appropriate, reworking it again if necessary.

As you work through your own journey of making flowers, you will no doubt come to find the papers that you most prefer working with or are most available to you. The papers below are some that I use the most, and we'll be working with them throughout the book.

180g Italian crepe paper (A)

This paper is the one that I use most often because of how versatile it is. Although it's the most heavyweight paper, it has a good amount of stretch, so can be used for everything from the tiniest of details to making huge, oversized flowers. There is a great range of colours as well. It comes in long rolls that are heavily textured due to the amount of stretch it has and there are machine lines running across the length. When I first started using it I thought it was too thick and heavy and wondered how I could make delicate flowers with it, but over time I have come to see it as a favourite.

160g German florist crepe paper (B)

Similar to the 180g paper, this is also a heavyweight paper, although the machine lines running across it are much less prominent. It has a slightly smoother texture but also a little less strength than the 180g. There is a good colour range, with some that you can't find elsewhere. I particularly like to use the greens in this paper as they are less prone to fading.

60g Italian crepe paper (C)

This has a lovely smooth texture compared to the heavier papers. It is much more lightweight and delicate and has an almost transparent quality in some colours. You can create really pretty blousy petals with this paper, although they are much more delicate as the paper doesn't have as much strength. It has a good colour range and I particularly like to use some of the greens for wrapping stems, as it can be less bulky than the heavier papers.

Doublette crepe paper (D)

This is a smooth and heavier 90g paper that is made by fusing together two sheets of lighter-weight crepe. It usually has two different colours to it, one on each side. They have no reference numbers on these papers, but the name of the paper is the two colours, i.e. olive/light olive. You might also see it referred to as 'double-sided' crepe paper. It's great to use if you need a smooth texture for a flower but also need the strength of a heavier weight as it holds a shape well. I use this paper most often either for petals or leaves. Doublette comes in smaller folds of paper rather than long rolls as with the other papers.

Other materials

Floral wire (A)

We build each paper flower around a piece of floral wire. This provides the central structure running through the stem to the top of the flower. As it's flexible we can give shape to the stem, bending it to mimic the natural gestures of the flower. You can use either bare-stem wire or paper-covered wire. I often like to use paper-covered wire for foliage because it grips more easily in intricate areas.

Wires come in different thicknesses called 'gauges'. The lower the gauge number, the thicker the wire. We most commonly use 18-gauge wire for a main flower stem, running up to 20, 22, 24, 26, 28 and 30. Green wires are most commonly used, but I sometimes use fine white wire for petals as well.

Leaves are usually placed around wire too, as this gives them support and ensures we can give more realistic shape to them. Often, we would use 24 and 26-gauge wire for leaves. You will also need a pair of wire cutters for cutting the wire.

When working with the floral wire it's best to try to keep it straight and only put pressure on it where you're working, because it can get bent as you work and then be difficult to get straight again.

Spool floral wire (B)

This is a much thinner wire that comes wound on a spool. I use it for helping me to make shapes on some flowers, as it can hold the paper very tightly.

Armature wire (C)

I use this for flowers with a very long stem and it comes in many gauges. It's quite soft and malleable, but as it comes in rolls you can achieve much longer stems with this. It's great for large flowers.

Chicken wire (D)

This wire mesh is great for giving structure to bouquets and installations of flowers.

Silk ribbon (E)

This is handy to have for adding to bouquets and wreaths for a pretty finishing touch.

Adhesives (F)

A glue that I would recommend using to make your flowers would be Aleene's Original Tacky Glue. In my day-to-day work, I use a small 18ml (0.66 fl oz) bottle of this glue and apply from this directly to the paper. I refill it from larger bottles when it runs out. It's similar to a PVA glue, but it dries a little faster, although not so fast that you can't reposition paper with it if you need to. One thing to be mindful of though is that it can dry on your hands as you work and then transfer on to the paper, so it's best to wash your hands if you see this happening.

I also use a spray adhesive to laminate paper (see laminating on page 19). The one I use is 3M CraftMount and it works well.

I also use a hot glue gun for certain tasks. See Tools on page 14.

Flower stamens (G)

These are pre-made stamens that are great to use for paper flowers, such as blossoms, and they are also used widely in making sugar flowers for cake decorating. These come with two stamens on each stem, one at each end. They are available in a wide range of colours and sizes. If you can't find the exact colour you need, you can colour white stamens yourself with paint or a marker pen.

Floral tape (H)

This is a thin tape used by florists that comes in different colours. When it is stretched it releases a glue and so this can be used for wrapping flower stems, although I use it mostly for making initial shapes. I often use it to make bud shapes.

Polystyrene/spun cotton balls/plastic beads (I)

These are great to give a round shape for flower centres like poppies and anemones and for berries and buds. I usually hot glue polystyrene to the floral wire to make sure it is secure. You can get them in different sizes from 1cm (0.4in) diameter upwards, but if I need a very tiny shape I will use plastic beads.

Colouring materials and how to use them

There are various materials and methods we can use to colour papers that mimic the graduated tones and details of the colours of real flowers. These are the colouring materials we'll be using in this book, which can make the flowers more realistic.

Soft pastels (1)

This is one of my favourite methods of colouring paper because it creates a lovely gradation of colour that is easy to apply and control. I use soft pastels as they give the most delicate results.

To colour paper with pastel: scrape the surface of the pastel with a scalpel (or other sharp object) to reduce a little of the pastel to a powder. I place the powdered pastel in a ceramic dish. You can then apply the pastel to the paper with a pastel sponge, or a cosmetic sponge wedge as they are less expensive. When working with pastels, less is more, so it's best to apply a little at a time and build up the layers if needed. You don't want any harsh lines of pastel on the paper, so be careful to blend the colour out to a subtle gradation with your sponge. My favourite brand of pastels to use is Sennelier, although PanPastels are excellent too and don't need to be reduced to a powder.

Pastel pencils (2)

These are great for applying thick, opaque colour in a very fine, controlled way to small areas.

To use the pencils: Apply the colour directly on to the paper and leave it as it is or blend with your finger. You can also blend it out with water and a paintbrush. Again, it's good to build the colour up with these gradually if you need to as it's easy to put too much on to the paper. To create a subtle blend of colour, use water on your paintbrush and keep washing the brush as you blend it out. I tend to use Conté á Paris pastel pencils but will use other brands too if I need a colour not in their range.

Liquid Watercolours (3)

These are a versatile medium for colouring papers and can be used to apply the lightest of washes and the loveliest deep applications of colour too.

To use the liquid watercolours: Dispense a few drops of the ink into a small container using the dropper applicator. Then with a watercolour paintbrush I apply a little to a scrap piece of paper to take away the excess and then apply a thin wash of colour to the paper. I then blend this out with just water on the paintbrush and continue to wash the brush to apply more water and blend the colour. I use Dr. Ph. Martin's Hydrus Watercolours as they are light-fast, archival-quality liquid watercolours

Tea staining

Staining paper with tea or coffee is very useful for reducing the brightness of some crepe papers and for staining white papers into a crispy beige.

To stain with tea: I make the tea quite strong in a suitably sized container, place the piece of paper into the tea bath and let the paper soak completely for about a minute, then remove it and let it dry naturally.

Marker pens (4)

Using alcohol-based markers is a great way to add small details to flower petals.

To use the markers: These markers will bleed when applied to the paper, so it's best to go slowly and work very finely. I usually use Winsor & Newton Promarkers.

Collage

We can also create a collage effect by layering pieces of crepe paper on to crepe paper to add colours and details to the flower pieces we make.

To collage paper: Cut out the pieces of collaged paper and then apply a very thin layer of tacky glue all over the back, smoothing over with your finger. Then place where it needs to be. A second way to do this is that if the pieces are very fine, you can apply the glue to the surface that you are attaching to first, smooth with your finger and then place the collaged piece on top.

Tools

Scissors (A)
I'm particularly fond of using a small pair of precision scissors for fine details; small 10cm (4in) Westcott scissors are excellent for fringing papers. For general cutting I use a standard pair of 18cm (7in) scissors, which I find is a good length to give enough control while I'm working.

Wire cutters (B)
These are essential for cutting floral wires. They are also a great tool for bending and making shapes with the wire.

Hot glue gun and glue sticks (C)
It's useful to have a glue gun to use if you're gluing anything other than paper, such as polystyrene balls, or if you're making oversized flowers and need a stronger glue to hold it all together.

Scalpel (not pictured)
I do find it useful to keep a scalpel nearby for working with pastel colouring which you'll find later in this book. I also sometimes use it if I find I need to strip down a wire because I've wrapped it too thickly.

Tweezers (D)
It's very handy to have a pair of these around for pinching paper when you need to. I find them great to have when making poppy and tulip centres. An inexpensive pair of cosmetic tweezers does the job for me.

Mechanical pencil (E)
I'm quite lost without my mechanical pencil when drafting and copying out templates. The very fine lead helps me to draft them as accurately as possible.

Ruler (F)
An essential for measuring when reading tutorials and making sure things are in proportion.

Paintbrushes (G)
Watercolour paintbrushes are the ones I tend to use the most, for watercolours and sometimes pastels. I particularly like a very short, small brush for fine details.

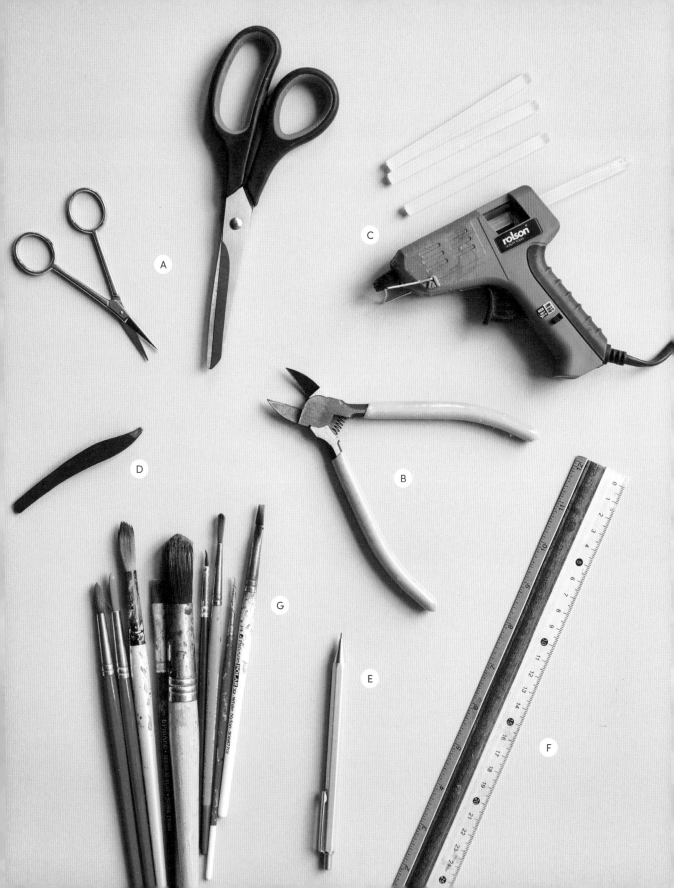

Techniques

Tips for working with crepe paper

Grain
When working with crepe for the first time, it's important to observe the grain, which is the direction the fibres are lying in to create the paper. (You can see in image 2 on page 18 that the grain runs from the top to the bottom of the piece of paper.)

Colour references
Manufacturers' reference numbers have been used where applicable, to ensure consistency when purchasing colours from different retailers. Where this isn't possible with some brands, colour names have been used instead.

Machine lines
Some of the heavier papers have machine lines running across the length of the roll of paper. I tend to avoid cutting templates with the line running across them if possible or to at least try to cut the

template so that the line sits in a less conspicuous place. If I can't avoid it at all then I work with it; they will often be reduced and flattened in the making process.

Don't use too much glue
It's best to avoid using too much glue as this can make things quite soggy and messy. Generally, a light amount of tacky glue smoothed over into a thin layer with your fingertip is more than enough to hold the paper.

Don't worry!
I've seen many people in my workshops being very tentative with the paper, worried that it will tear. I will let you in to a secret – the paper is more robust than it looks and if it does happen to tear, you can always re-cut a template if you need to.

Techniques for working with crepe paper

Accordion folding (1)
This is a great time-saving technique for cutting multiple flower parts and involves folding the paper behind the template several times before cutting the layers all at once. This helps us to cut multiple pieces in one go. If you're making a flower that has a lot of petals, it can save a lot of time, rather than cutting each one individually. You just need to be careful to not cut too many at once as you can lose detail. To accordion fold your paper you will need to cut a strip of crepe that covers the height of your template and gives enough length to cut several petals at once.

1

Stretching (2)

This technique involves taking the paper between both hands and pulling your hands and the paper apart, stretching the paper out. This makes the paper thinner and smoother. It often means we can cut more detail in to the paper, and it makes the flower look prettier. It's particularly used with the heavier papers. You can either stretch the paper fully or in part, depending on what you're trying to achieve. Stretching the paper can result in the colour becoming less intense and the machine lines will also become a little less visible.

Removing grain (3)

A second way to reduce the textured grain of the heavyweight paper is by scraping the surface of the paper with your thumbnail. I use this on small pieces of crepe. To do this, take the piece of crepe between your hands with the grain running horizontally. Then with your prominent hand, scrape the surface with your thumbnail, while holding the paper underneath your thumb with your forefinger. You can repeat this several times if you need a very smooth surface.

Fluting (4)

This involves giving a little wave to the edge of the paper, often to a petal. To flute the edge of the paper, hold the paper at the edge with both hands and with the left hand push the paper back, with the right hand push the paper forwards (almost as if you're trying to tear the edge of the paper but not going through with it). This results in a small tight wave in the petal edge. You can flute along the whole edge of a petal. I sometimes also use the same principle to flute petals with more of my fingers to give shape to a larger area such as an entire petal rather than just the edge.

Fringing (5)

Fringing is a great technique for making tiny, detailed stamens and flower centres that can be really effective when the fringed paper is rolled together. Sometimes it's necessary to use small precision scissors to cut a very fine fringe. Generally, the finer the fringe you can cut into the paper, the better the flower will look. One of my tips for achieving a very fine fringe would be to steady your hands as much as possible. When I'm doing this, I will often rest my scissor blades carefully on top of my fingers of my opposite hand. This helps to steady my hands and the crepe and produce a finer fringe.

6

7

8

9

Cupping (6)

This involves giving a round dome shape to a piece of paper, often for shaping petals. To do this, take the paper between both hands at the point that you want to be shaped. Gently stretch the paper over the curve of the back of both of your thumbs. You can cup the paper deeply or lightly. This can take a little practise at first. Be careful with lighter-weight papers that you don't stretch the paper too much and keep your fingernails away as well, as this can create visible stretch marks in the paper.

Curling (7)

I often use the closed blades of a small pair of scissors to gently give a slight curl to the edge of a piece of paper. I also sometimes use a short piece of 18-gauge floral wire to give an even tighter curl. You can curl the paper either upwards or downwards.

Pleating (8)

To tightly pleat petals, I take a cut petal, apply a thin line of glue close to the bottom, then smooth over with my finger. I then place the petal on a smooth surface, push against the edge of the petal with both thumbs, then with my fingernails I gather the paper in tiny amounts all the way along to the end. The smaller the amounts you gather, the tighter the pleat. Then gather the paper at the very bottom and twist a little to hold together. To pleat paper loosely or in one place, for example one pleat in the centre of a petal, I pick up the petal in my fingers and with my right hand I gather the paper and fold over a small amount to form a pleat.

Laminating (9)

It can be handy to thicken a particular crepe paper by gluing two or more pieces together. This might be because you prefer a particular colour, but the paper won't hold enough weight for what you need. You can laminate paper by gluing the pieces together with tacky glue that is thinly dotted and evenly spread across the surface using your fingertips. Firmly smooth and press together both pieces of paper. This is a good technique for small areas. It's important that the glue is spread over the whole surface so that the two pieces don't come away from each other when you cut them. A second way to laminate paper is to use a spray adhesive such as 3M Craft Mount. This is better for gluing together larger areas. You can also use iron-on fusible webbing, although this isn't a method that I've used personally.

Techniques for making stems and leaves

Making stems and leaves and attaching them together are techniques that we use for most of the flowers throughout the book. Often when I'm making a flower, the piece really comes to life when the foliage is completed. It is well worth spending time on this, even though it may seem less interesting in some ways than making the flower head. There are several ways of making foliage, some with more detail than others.

HOW TO WRAP A MAIN FLOWER STEM

This involves using strips of crepe paper to wrap around and cover the bare wire in the stems we make, to make them thicker and more realistic. We also cover the excess paper underneath the flower head and the base of the petals..

1 To wrap a main flower stem, take a 1cm (0.4in) wide strip of the crepe paper specified in your flower tutorial. Cut the strip across the grain of the crepe paper rather than in the same direction of it, so that the grain runs down the width of the strip. Stretch the paper strip out fully between both hands, then apply a light amount of glue to the top of the strip. Smooth this out with your fingers into a light layer.

2 Glue the strip horizontally around the base of the flower, covering the base of the petals. Then bring the strip down on an angle to cover any remaining excess paper, applying another light layer of glue when it has run out. Then continue this down the wire stem, keeping the strip in your left hand and on a 45° angle, turning the wire clockwise with your right. It helps to keep your hands close together when you wrap to give you more control.

3 Continue to wrap on the angle down the stem to the end. The aim is to cover the stem with as little paper as possible so that it doesn't get bulky, so make sure you are continually making progress down the stem. If at any point the strip breaks or runs out, you can simply glue that piece down and start again from the same point with another. Once you reach the end you can tear the strip and glue it down.

4 Repeat the layers on the wire stem as many times as stipulated in the tutorial.

2

Ways to make a leaf

LEAVES WITH NO WIRE

The easiest way to make a leaf is to make a leaf with no wire at all to support it. An example would be a tulip leaf. You can simply cut the leaf template out of the green crepe paper with the grain running down the length of the leaf. A little glue can then be applied to the base, and this can then be placed directly on to the stem. Sometimes it is necessary to hide the base of the leaf by wrapping a strip of crepe paper over the base with a little glue. This can also provide extra security to keep the leaf attached to the stem.

1-2

3

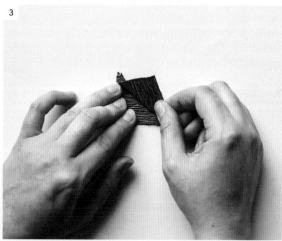

WIRED LEAVES ON THE BIAS

This gives a realistic leaf where the grain of the paper runs diagonally in opposite directions from the centre of the leaf, as you often get in nature. You can see examples of this kind of leaf in the Rose leaves on pages 24. The leaf is also strengthened because it has a thin wire running through it so it is also easier to style realistically. When attaching these wired leaves to flowers and other leaves it's best to position the glued seam facing to the back and show off the prettiest front side of the leaf.

To create this leaf with single colour papers

1 Take a piece of the required crepe paper and if using heavyweight papers, stretch out about one-third (so you don't stretch the paper all the way). If you're using lighter-weight papers then you don't need to stretch it. Cut a square piece that more than covers the size of your template when placed on the diagonal.

2 Cut the square in half on the diagonal as straight as you can. Place the two cut triangles on top of each other with the grain on both running 45-degrees to the left (see image 4-5 opposite). Apply a fine line of glue to the long edge of the top piece on the inside and wipe away any excess. Glue this down, 2mm (0.08in) from the top edge of the lower piece. Pinch both pieces together taking care to ensure they're fully glued.

3 Once dry, open the pieces so the grain is running upwards and then push down on the right side and fold a seam along the glued edge. Cut out the

4

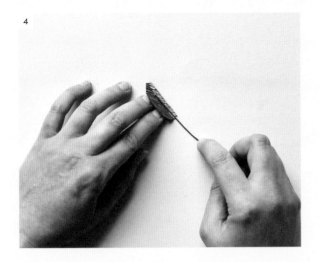

template leaf shape, centering the template in the middle of the fold and ensuring the grain runs in the direction of the arrows on the template. Cut tiny notches with the precision scissors into the sides of the leaves if needed for your flower.

4 To place a wire in the leaf, open the seam at the back and place a light layer of glue down it. With your finger, spread this over the whole seam. Then take your floral wire (24 or 26-gauge wire as specified in the flower tutorial) and lay this three-quarters up the seam, placing it right into the inner fold. Push the leaf down and then push down all the way along the seam to properly secure. Trim any excess paper at the base of the leaf if needed to create a consistent shape.

4–5

6

To create this leaf with doublette crepe paper
Doublette paper has a different colour on each side. You will need to cut your squares slightly differently to make a wired leaf in this paper.

1 Cut two squares of doublette crepe paper that are larger than your leaf template.

2 Place them both on a table with the colour that you would like the flower to be facing upwards.

3 Cut both on the diagonal, but we need them to be cut on opposite diagonals to each other this time.

4 Take one triangle of crepe paper from one square and the same corresponding triangle from the other square. You can save the remaining two pieces to make another leaf later if you need to.

5 Follow the previous tutorial for gluing the two pieces together and then the remaining steps as well. Although make sure the colour that you would like your leaf to be is in the centre, with both sides that have the same colour touching when you glue them down.

6 Once the pieces are dry, you can then open them out in the same way as the previous tutorial and make your leaf in the same way.

How to make a multiple-leaf sprig

Some flowers such as roses and dahlias have multiple leaflets making up one larger leaf. I'm going to use the example of a rose leaf to show how to put one of these leaves together. You'll also need to check any specific instructions for the leaves of the flower you're making in the individual tutorials.

1 Gather the required leaflets you've made following the previous leaves tutorial and any instructions in the flower tutorial too. Take the main leaf at the end of the sprig first. Cut a 5mm (0.2in) strip of the required crepe paper stated in the flower tutorial (this is often the 160g German crepe in grass green).

2 Stretch out the strip fully and with a light layer of glue at the end, wrap around at the base of the main leaf. On a 45-degree angle, continue down the wire, wrapping tightly and gently to not bend the wire. Turn the leaf stem with your right hand and bring the strip down the wire with your left.

3 Check your flower instructions to see how far down the wire you need to wrap until you need to put the next leaflet in. At this point stop and ensure the next leaflets' stems have been bent 45 degrees so that they will sit flush on the stem on the side of the sprig that they need to be placed on.

4 With a light amount of glue at the top of the wire on the next leaflets, place both leaflets on and next to the strip so that when the strip is next wound round, it secures the leaflets' wire snugly at the right place.

5 Continue to wrap around the crepe strip until the point when you need to place in another leaf. Ensure that you keep the multiple wires as straight as possible.

6 Repeat the placing of the next set of leaflets if needed. Then continue to wrap again, until you reach the point where the leaf will join the main stem as per the flower instructions. At this stage you can tear the crepe paper strip just below this point and glue it down.

7 Bend the stems of the sprig 45 degrees downwards so that they will sit flush on the main stem of the flower. Cut the individual floral wires down in a staggered way at different points to reduce bulk on the main stem.

1

2

4

How to attach a leaf to a stem

We use the same principle to attach leaves to stems as we do to attach leaflets to leaf sprigs.

Apply a little glue to the top of the bent leaf sprig stem. When you have wrapped the main flower stem as needed, place the leaf sprig on the stem following any placement stated in the flower tutorial.

Take a 1cm (0.4in) strip of the stem crepe paper and with a light layer of glue, wrap around the leaf sprig and the main stem, to conceal the leaf wires and hold the leaf in place. Continue wrapping down the stem, adding any other leaves if needed, to the end. If there are bumps on the stem from the wires of the leaves, you can wrap the stem again to hide these and make the stem a consistent width. I sometimes wrap from directly below the wires to try to even the stem out.

The flowers

Now that we've gone through the materials and techniques we are going to use, we can now move on to putting these into practice and taking our first steps with making some flowers. We move through the seasons with the tutorials, starting with the quiet beauty of winter and spring and then progress through to the colourful showiness of the heights of summer. I hope you enjoy connecting with your hands and the materials to make something beautiful.

Cyclamen

These are one of my absolute favourite winter flowers, and with their distinctive shape they look like they could be from another world. Red cyclamen are beautiful at Christmas and make a stunning table decoration. You could also experiment with different colours and make an array of pink, purple and white blooms.

You will need

180g Italian crepe paper in mustard 579, burgundy 588 and brown 613

60g Italian crepe paper in magenta 212 or red 312

Doublette crepe paper in olive/light olive

20-gauge floral wire

Spool floral wire

24-gauge paper-covered floral wire

Winsor & Newton Promarker in burgundy

White pastel pencil

Sennelier soft pastel in brown 061

Standard scissors and precision scissors

Card, tracing paper and pencil for templates (see page 170)

Ruler

Smooth-sided pencil or pen (with no ridges), approximately 9mm (0.4in) in diameter

Aleene's Original Tacky Glue

Pastel or cosmetic sponge

Scalpel and ceramic dish

Wire cutters

To make the stamen and stem

1 Take a 5cm (0.2in) deep strip of 180g mustard crepe paper cut against the grain, stretch out fully and wrap around the top 3cm (1.2in) of the 20-gauge floral wire stem, bringing the strip down on a 45-degree angle as you glue. Tear this and glue down once you have covered 3cm (1.2in).

2 Then cut a 5.5 x 5cm (2.2 x 2in) rectangle of 180g burgundy crepe paper against the grain as well as a second piece that measures 6 x 2cm (2.4 x 0.8in).

3 Fully stretch out both rectangles of paper between your fingers. With the larger piece, fold over lengthways and press down firmly along the fold line. Apply a thin layer of glue all over the inside of one side of the fold and press down firmly to secure the folded paper together. Repeat with the second smaller piece, but this time repeat the process twice again with the paper, until you have a very thin strip of glued-together paper.

4 Apply a thin layer of glue to the top (folded edge) of the larger strip and glue down the thin strip of paper to the top edge. Press down very firmly all the way along so the pieces fuse together.

5 Wrap the final strip firmly around the pencil and cut at the point where there will be an overlap to glue the two edges of the rolled paper together.

6 While the piece is still wrapped around the pencil, apply a thin layer of glue to the right edge and stick down to close the roll around the pencil. Slide the paper cylinder off the end.

7 Take your 20-gauge floral wire and apply a little glue around the paper-covered wire, 1cm (0.40in) from the top. Place the rolled paper over the top so the end of the wire and the top of the rolled paper are level.

8 With a piece of spool floral wire, wrap tightly round the rolled paper and the wire at about the halfway point a few times to secure in place. With the closed point of the precision scissors, tease the rolled paper on the inside into a neat, round shape. Let dry for a few minutes, then remove the piece of wire.

1

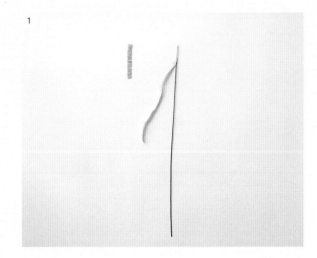

3

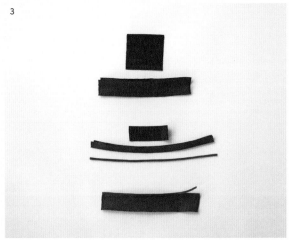

5

8

To make the petals.

10 Cut five petals for each flower from the 60g crepe paper of your choice, ensuring the grain of the paper matches the markers on the template. Using your thumb and the side of your forefinger, scrape your thumbnail down the length of the petal to give a little movement.

11 Add a light layer of glue at the bottom of each petal (I also smooth this over with my finger), attach the first petal, folding the bottom 2mm (0.08in) of the petal inside the circle of paper. Repeat with the rest of the petals, placing them tightly together so they sit evenly around the bottom of the rolled centre. Pinch the paper together around the bottom of each petal. I also use the precision scissor points to smooth the paper inside the centre circle.

12 Next, bend the flower-head right over at the top, just underneath the flower (I use wire cutters to grip the stem near the flower-head to do this, without cutting through the wire).

13 With the marker pen, very gently add a little colour to the base of each petal in very light, small strokes.

14 You can then twist each of the petals gently around on themselves to give them some shape.

9 Cut away a little of the bottom of the burgundy paper with your precision scissors to reduce the bulk. Then using a thin 1cm (0.40in) strip of the 180g brown crepe paper, wrap the full stem three times on a 45-degree angle, adding a little glue here and there to secure. You can see the instructions on page 20 to see how to do this. Make sure that you cover the excess burgundy paper too, but just once so that it doesn't appear too thick in comparison with the stem.

11

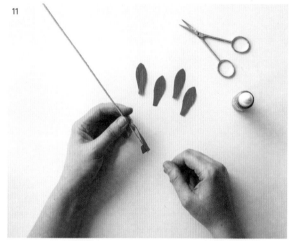

13

To make the leaves

15 Cut two squares 6 x 6cm (2.4 x 2.4in) of olive/light olive doublette crepe paper and make one of each of the leaves following the instructions on page 23. With these leaves however, the grain needs to run down the leaf, as per the arrows on the leaf templates. You will need to make sure the grain runs the correct way before you cut it out.

16 Apply a thin layer of glue along the seam at the back and wipe the excess away with your finger. Take a 24-gauge paper-covered wire and place inside the seam, then press together to secure.

17 With a white pastel pencil, add details to the leaf in a heart shape with short firm strokes. If you apply them with the strokes running in line with the grain of the paper, it's easier. Then take a 5mm (0.2in) strip of brown crepe paper and wrap it 2cm (0.8in) down the stem of the leaf on a 45-degree angle; tear the paper off and glue down. Repeat again to make the second leaf.

18 To add the leaves to the stem, take an 8mm (0.3in) wide strip of brown crepe paper and stretch between your fingers, then apply a little glue to the end.

19 Cut the leaf wires 5mm (0.2in) from the end of the crepe paper and bend the wire to an angle so that it will sit flush on the side of the stem. Apply a little glue and place on the lower part of the stem, wrapping with a strip of paper to cover the wires and secure. Tear and glue down the paper at the end. Repeat with another wrap if the wires are very noticeable through the paper.

20 You can now style the flower and shape the stem of your paper cyclamen and then twist the petals round on themselves to give the shape as if they are being blown back in the wind.

21 You can now apply some of the brown pastel to the stem of the flower and leaves to darken it to give that final touch (see page 12 for how to use pastels).

17

19

Anemone de Caen 'Bicolour'

With their distinctive red rings, these are one of my favourite varieties of anemone. I really enjoy using pastel pencils to get the colouring just right, although if you are a beginner, you could try making them without the colouring at first. I also use some watercolour to age the edges of the petals slightly, but this is optional.

You will need

180g Italian crepe paper in cream 17A1, black 602 and green 622

160g German florist crepe paper in grass green

18-gauge floral wire

1cm (0.4in) polystyrene ball

Stabilo Carbothello pastel pencil in carmine red 325

Dr. Ph. Martin's Hydrus Watercolor in raw sienna 32H (optional)

Standard scissors and precision scissors

Card, tracing paper and pencil for templates (see page 170)

Ruler

Wire cutters

Aleene's Original Tacky Glue

Hot glue and glue gun

Small watercolour paintbrush and water jar

To make the centre

1 Cut a rectangle of 180g cream crepe paper across the grain measuring 9 x 4cm (3.5 x 1.6in) and stretch fully between your fingers.

2 Next, cut three thin strips of 180g black crepe paper across the grain, measuring 5mm (0.2in) deep and 9cm (3.5in) long and stretch each between your fingers too.

3 Apply tacky glue all along the top edge of the cream piece and smooth over the glue with your finger. Then press the stretched black strip down along the top edge of the cream strip. Repeat again covering the black strip with a second layer. Make sure the strip is firmly glued down. Then turn over and glue down a strip to the top of the other side. Firmly press the pieces together and set aside to dry.

4 With a little hot glue, place a polystyrene ball on to the end of a piece of 18-gauge floral wire, making sure the wire doesn't go all the way through.

5 Take a 1.5 x 2.5cm (0.6 x 1in) rectangle of 180g black crepe paper and stretch between your fingers. Place a thin layer of glue over the black piece, smoothing with your finger and then place over the top of the polystyrene, gathering around and twisting underneath, adding a little more glue if needed.

1-3

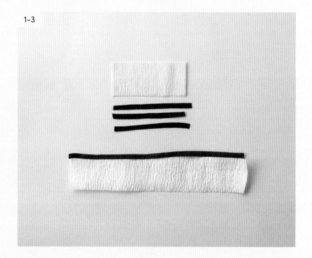

4-6

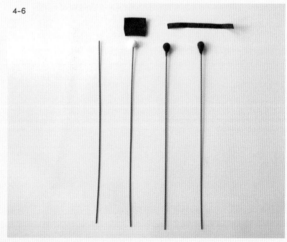

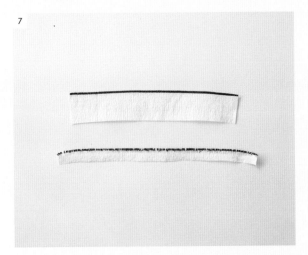

7

9

6 Then take a 4.5cm x 6mm (1.8 x 0.24in) strip of black crepe paper, stretch out, and with a light layer of glue wrap around tightly underneath the polystyrene to create a ledge for the petals to sit on.

7 Now we can go back to the cream and black strip we prepared earlier once it is dry. Trim this down, cutting the width of the black strip at the top to 2mm (0.08in) and then trimming each side down so it is even. Then fringe this piece as finely as you can using precision scissors 5mm (0.2in) of the way down the piece starting at the top with the black (see fringing on page 18). When you have fringed all the way along, you can then twist the fringe between your fingers to create a little texture. Dampening your fingers very slightly can help to get a good grip on the paper.

8 Trim down the cream piece along the bottom of the fringe, leaving a 1cm (0.4in) gap from the bottom of the fringe.

9 Apply a little glue to the bottom-left corner, smooth over with your finger and wrap this around the centre tightly and evenly, with the top of the fringe sitting 1 to 2mm (0.04 to 0.08in) above the top of the black, round centre. Keep applying a little more glue as you go and smoothing it over with your finger, then secure at the end.

10 Use your fingers to splay out the fringing from the centre and trim down the lower layers with precision scissors, so that there are no stray pieces of fringe and the centre looks uniform.

To make the petals

11 Cut an 8 x 6cm (3.1 x 2.4in) piece of 180g cream crepe paper, fully stretch out between your fingers and cut out three petals from the first petal template and four from each of the other sizes. You will need to cut a second piece of crepe paper to cut them all out. With your precision scissors, scrape the closed blades down the surface of each petal on each side to flatten the grain.

12 Take your red pastel pencil and the template for the red circle. Place the template with the straight edge in line with the bottom of the petal, with the centre of the template in the centre of the petal. Using firm, small strokes with the pastel pencil, stroke away from the top of the template to create the curve of red across each petal. You can vary slightly the length of the strokes you make. You can practise the colouring on a spare piece of crepe paper beforehand if you prefer.

13 Take a paintbrush and dip in water, then gently brush out the colour from the very top edge of the red circle so that it fades out to very light pink and then to the cream of the paper. You can keep washing and adding water to your brush to fade the colour out. Then dampen the red pastel at the bottom to smooth the colour out slightly. You can then add a few tiny strokes of the pencil at the bottom of the line to give some stronger colour. Repeat with each petal.

14 Once each petal is dry, take your precision scissors and subtly cut tiny waves and the occasional curved notch into each petal to make each very subtly different. Then gather each petal to a point at the base and apply a little glue.

15 Starting with one of the smallest petals and working your way through to adding the largest petals last, place the small petals equally around the centre, directly below but not on top of the fringe of the centre. Add them all at the same level. Place the medium petals on next, overlapping them a little behind the smallest petals. You can fill any gaps with the largest petals. All the petals need to be added at exactly the same height so that the red ring line matches up around the flower. If you need to, you can always reposition a petal. Press each firmly underneath the flower to ensure they stay in place.

12

13

15
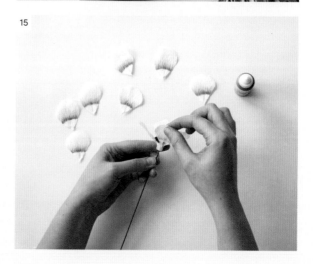

17

20

To make the stem and leaves

16 Using wire cutters, cut down the main stem wire if you wish to have a shorter flower.

17 Following the instructions on page 20, wrap the wire stem starting at the top of the bare wire with a strip of 1cm (0.4in) wide stretched-out 180g green crepe paper. I repeat this around six times to get a good thickness on the stem. Then wrap a shorter piece around directly underneath the flower-head to cover the excess paper.

18 To make a leaf, cut a square of 160g grass-green crepe paper 4 x 6cm (1.6 x 2.4in) and scrape along the surface to flatten the grain over the closed blades of your precision scissors. Cut round the leaf template. Repeat to make around seven leaves in total. You can cut a little more detail into each leaf to make them a little different to each other if you prefer.

19 Place a little glue at the very bottom of your leaf and twist between your fingers to gather the leaf together at the bottom. Glue to the stem roughly 3 to 4cm (1.2 to 1.6in) from the base of the flower.

20 Wrap the stem one last time with one of the stem strips to cover the ends of the leaves on the stem and then down to the bottom.

21 You can now bend the stem to style your paper anemone and adjust the flower centre and the petals and bring down the leaves. Curve the edges of the leaves both up and down using the closed blades of your precision scissors. You can add a very diluted amount of watercolour to the edges of a few of the petals to give an aged effect and break up the colour, but this is optional.

Crocus bulb

It's always great to see these beauties unfurl their petals to signal the end of winter. They have a real delicacy and make a lovely addition to the base of a spring arrangement. If you are looking to make your first flowers these make a great starter flower, especially if you make them on a stem instead of with a bulb.

You will need

60g Italian crepe paper in orange 294
180g Italian crepe paper in lilac 592 and cream 17A1
Doublette crepe paper in olive/light olive
20-gauge floral wire
Conté pastel pencil in yellow 004
Sennelier soft pastel in violet 311
Standard scissors and precision scissors
Card, tracing paper and pencil for templates (see page 170)
Ruler
Aleene's Original Tacky Glue
Wire cutters

To also make a bulb

1.5cm (0.6in) polystyrene ball
Brown and black watercolour paint
Hot glue and glue gun
Scalpel
Pastel or cosmetic sponges and ceramic dish
Watercolour paintbrush and water jar

To make the centre

1 Cut a piece of 20-gauge floral wire to the length that you would like your crocus flower to be (these are around 10 to 13cm (4 to 5in)).

2 Cut a piece of 60g orange crepe paper 1 x 2.5cm (0.4 x 1in) with the grain running vertically and gently stretch the paper with your fingers.

3 Cut a slant on each side of the paper, then add a very light layer of glue to the paper, leaving a few millimetres (0.1in) free of glue at the top.

4 Place the floral wire down the centre of the paper a few millimetres (0.1in) from the top and wrap the paper around, pinching evenly into place with a light layer of glue.

5 Next, take another piece of 60g orange crepe paper of the same size, stretch between your fingers as before and then cut two slits lengthways, two-thirds of the way down, to form three fringed pieces. Apply a little glue to the fringes only and smooth over with your fingers. Take each piece of fringe between your fingers and twist. The glue will keep each twisted piece together.

6 Glue the fringed piece around the covered wire, placing the top of the fringe a few millimetres (0.1in) below the top of the paper on the floral wire. Try to ensure the three pieces are evenly spaced.

7 Take a strip of 60g orange crepe paper cut 5mm (0.2in) wide against the grain. Stretch between your fingers, apply a little glue to the end and start to wrap around the wire at the bottom of the fringed pieces. Continue to wrap around, concentrating on the centre of your wrapping to create an oval shape measuring about 4mm (0.2in) across at the widest point.

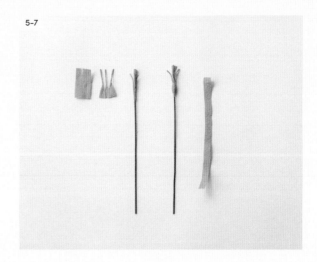

To make the petals

8 Cut six petals for each flower. Take a piece of 4.5 x 5cm (1.8 x 2in) 180g lilac crepe paper and stretch out to 7.5cm (3in). Cut three petals out from the template and repeat again to cut the six needed. Reduce the grain of the paper by holding each petal with your hands, then with your thumb and forefinger scrape your fingernail down the surface of the paper. Cup each petal deeply in the centre, following the instructions on page 19. Lay the template on each petal again and trim round to remove any excess.

9 To add the shaded violet colour to each petal, follow the pastel shading instructions on page 12, adding a very light amount of colour to the top edge and blending out on both sides of the petal. Then add yellow pastel pencil to the base of the petal on the inside, with firm strokes in a half-diamond shape.

10 Place a light coating of glue at the bottom of each petal, then take a petal and glue to the centre, in the centre of the oval shape that you've made. Place the next two petals around the centre, level with the first. They should all be evenly spaced. Add the remaining three petals so that they overlap the first three covering in-between each of the three gaps. Pinch the petals at the bottom to secure. If you don't wish to add a bulb, jump to step 12.

11 To add a bulb, hot glue a polystyrene ball to the bottom of the floral wire, without piercing the base of the polystyrene.

8

9

10

10

To make the stem, bulb and leaves

12 Cut a strip of 180g cream crepe paper 8mm (0.3in) wide, stretch between your fingers, and wrap the stem following the instructions on page 20. Continue to the bottom of the wire or to the top of the bulb, then tear the paper, glue down and pinch to secure.

13 We need a tapered thickness on the stem, from thin on the top to thicker at the bottom. Wrapping with the strips of paper needs to be repeated to build up the layers. After the first few layers, start off from different points around the centre of the stem, wrapping to achieve a consistent increase. As a guide, the flowers I've made have tended to have a thickness of 2 to 3mm (0.08 to 0.1in) at the top and 4 to 5mm (0.2in) at the bottom of the stem. You may need to increase the thickness of the wrapping strip as the stem gets thicker.

14 Once you are happy with your stem, you can then wrap around the polystyrene ball (if you're using one) to completely cover it using the same technique and adding a little more glue to the strip as you wrap the strip around.

15 To add the leaves, cut thin, tapered pieces of olive, light olive doublette crepe paper. These tend to be around 6 to 7cm (2.4 to 2.8in) long and I cut around three to five per flower. Apply a light amount of glue to the bottom half of each leaf and place around the stem. They should sit a little way underneath the flower-head.

16 Take a 1cm (0.4in) strip of 180g cream crepe paper and stretch out, then wrap around starting about 3cm (1.2in) below the top of the leaves on a 45-degree angle. Wrap to the bottom keeping the leaves flat against the stem.

11-13

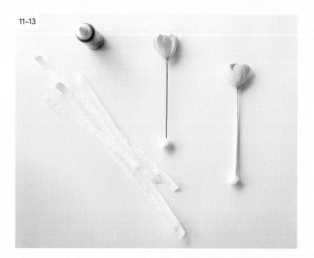

15-16

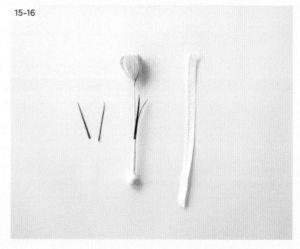

17 Now we can work on the roots. Cut a piece of 180g cream crepe paper 1.5 x 4cm (0.6 x 1.6in) with the grain running vertically and stretch fully out. Fringe it in approximately 2mm (0.08in) wide pieces, leaving about 1cm (0.4in) at the top un-fringed (see page 18 for instructions on fringing paper.) Apply glue dots over the strands and smooth over with your finger, then twist each piece together into a thin strand and let dry.

18 Apply glue to the un-fringed paper and wrap the roots around the base of the bulb in a tight circle so that they sit closely together. With your fingernails, push the base of the roots firmly together. Cut some strands down a little so they aren't all the same length.

19 To colour the bulb, use brown watercolour paint mixed with a little black. I find it's best to build up the colour gradually, so I start with a lighter colour and then add a little black to the colour, darkening the bulb particularly around the bottom. You can add paint to the root pieces too. I also add a little paint up the stem, smudging with my finger.

20 As one of the finishing touches I add a little yellow pastel on a sponge to the ridge around the bottom of the flower-head.

21 To style the flower I place a gentle bend in the stem. You can open up the petals so that they are wide open or leave them closed.

Narcissus triandrus

This narcissus has an ethereal, fairy-tale quality. Its colours vary from cream to yellow so you can choose which colours you prefer. It's one of the simpler flowers to make, so a good beginner flower if you're just starting out with your making. You could also add a bulb to these, see pages 43–45 if you would like to do that.

You will need

180g Italian crepe paper in cream 17A1 and yellow 574/575
Doublette crepe paper in white/vanilla, light yellow/yellow and olive/light olive
160g German florist crepe paper in grass green
60g Italian crepe paper in green 264 and white 330
20-gauge floral wire
Green spool floral wire
Standard scissors and precision scissors
Card, tracing paper and pencil for templates (see page 174)
Ruler
Wire cutters
Aleene's Original Tacky Glue
Tea and container for staining

To make the centre

1 Take a 5mm (0.2in) strip of 180g cream or yellow crepe paper, depending on which flower colour you choose. Stretch between your fingers and apply a light layer of glue. Wrap around the top of a piece of 20-gauge floral wire and down the stem on a 45-degree angle covering the top 2cm (0.8in) then cut and glue down.

2 Then cut a second piece of the same crepe paper measuring 3 x 3cm (1.2 x 1.2in). Stretch out fully and then cut down the piece to 1.5 x 2.5cm (0.6 x 1in). Then cut three even lines into this piece 1.5cm (0.6in) deep. Apply a light layer of glue and twist each strand together between your fingers to create four thin strands. Then apply a little glue across the base of the strands and glue around the central wire so all the pieces are at the same height.

3 To make the trumpet piece, take a 5 x 5cm (2 x 2in) piece of the 180g cream or yellow crepe paper of your choice and stretch this out fully. Fold over the left-hand edge by 4cm (1.6in) and place the centre template left-hand edge (marked by the dotted line) flush against the edge of the fold of the paper. Cut out and then unfold and flute the uneven top edge of the piece, following the instructions on page 18.

4 Take the left-hand side of the piece and apply a light line of glue to the very edge of the paper (on the other side) and glue the other side down on to this to form the trumpet shape.

5 Apply glue around the stamen paper 1cm (0.40in) from the bottom and place the trumpet over the top. It should sit level with the stamens. Gather the base together lightly and wrap around a piece of green spool floral wire tightly a few times about 3mm (0.1in) from the bottom to secure. With your little finger, gently tease the top and bottom out into a full shape trying to flatten out as many creases at the base of the shape as possible.

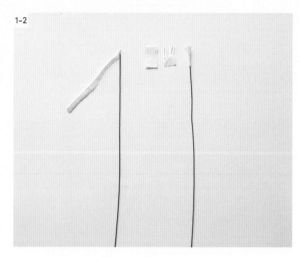

1–2

5

5

7

9

To make and attach the petals

6 Cut a 5cm (2in) wide strip of the white/vanilla or light yellow/yellow doublette crepe paper of your choice. Cut out six of the petal templates.

7 To shape each petal, hold each one between your fingers and twist round on itself.

8 To attach the petals, apply a little glue to the base of each petal on the side of the colour you want to face outwards. Remove the spool wire from around the trumpet.

9 Apply the first three petals at the ten, two and six o'clock points and then add the remaining petals in-between. Pinch underneath with your fingernails to secure them in place.

10 To ensure the petals sit evenly around the centre and attach well, you can place a small amount of glue underneath the trumpet and then with your little finger, push down inside the shape to secure it to the petals, readjusting if you need to as you go.

11 Repeat the above to make another bloom or two to sit on the same stem if you like.

To make the stem

12 Take a 7mm (0.3in) strip of 160g green crepe paper, stretch out fully and place a light layer of glue on the end. Then on a 45-degree angle, wrap down the stem covering the top 2 to 2.5cm (0.8 to 1in), then wrap backwards again and up to the top, repeating this and focusing on the top half more, so that the result is a long, tapered shape that's wider at the top.

13 Then take a 3mm (0.1in) strip of 60g green crepe paper and with a light layer of glue, wrap this around again and again underneath the tapered piece to create a short, fat oval shape.

14 You can now cut the wire stem down to a shorter length if you prefer. Then cut another strip of 160g

green crepe paper measuring 7mm (0.3in) wide and wrap down the length of the stem to the end, following the instructions on page 20. Repeat the wrap of the stem until it is around 2mm (0.08in) thick.

15 To make the spathe (the brown crispy piece at the top of the stem), take a 7 x 7cm square (2.8 x 2.8in) of 60g white crepe paper and stain this with strong tea (instructions on page 13). Once dry, cut out one piece for each flower using the petal template. Scrunch this together in your fingers and then unravel it.

16 Bend each of the flower stems down at an angle underneath the oval piece and place them together so that they are all at very slightly different heights. Take a 1cm (0.4in) wide strip of 160g grass-green crepe paper and with a light layer of glue, wrap several stems together if you like, enclosing the spathe at the top with the strip. Keep the stems as straight as possible as you wrap. Repeat the wrapping of the stem again, although we will use the 60g green crepe paper this time.

17 To make the leaves, cut long, thin, tapered leaves from the olive/light olive doublette crepe paper freehand with the grain running down the length. These should measure around 14 to 17 cm (5.5 to 6.7in) in length. Cut out two leaves and glue with a light layer of glue at the base of each leaf. Place these opposite each other on the stem, covering the base of them with a wrap of the 60g green crepe paper. You can now style the flower; curving the petals backwards and rearranging the flower-heads if needed and giving a very subtle curve to the stem.

13

16

17

Fuchsia

I adore the prettiness of these flowers and they never fail to make me smile. This is a slightly more complex piece to make, although it is well worth the time, so tackle this when you're feeling confident with your making. It's good to put more variety in to it too, so feel free to make this one your own and vary the size and placement of the flowers and leaves.

You will need

180g Italian crepe paper in red 586, purple 593, dark green 591 and burgundy 588
Doublette crepe paper in olive/ light olive
Red 1mm (0.04in) matt flower stamens
24 and 26-gauge paper-covered floral wire
18-gauge floral wire
White pastel pencil
Standard scissors and precision scissors
Card, tracing paper and pencil for templates (see page 174)
Ruler
Wire cutters
Aleene's Original Tacky Glue

We will need to make eight flowers, three to four buds and 15 leaves in total for a 45cm (18in) branch.

To make a single flower

1 Take four or five flower stamens, hold them together and bring one stamen 1cm (0.4in) lower than the others. Then cut straight across the stamens with scissors so that all the bottom stamens are removed.

2 Take a 5mm (0.20in) wide strip of 180g red crepe paper and stretch between your fingers. Apply a light layer of glue to the top of the strip and fold over the top of a piece of 24-gauge paper-covered floral wire on a 45-degree angle.

3 Place the stamens on the strip so that about 4cm (1.6in) of them hang over the end of the wire, applying a little glue. Wrap the strip around tightly to cover the end of the stamens and then tear the strip and glue down.

4 Next, stretch an 8 x 4cm (3.1 x 1.6in) piece of the 180g purple crepe paper and cut five petals per flower using the petal template, ensuring the grain runs in the direction of the arrows on the template.

5 Place a light, thin layer of glue on the thin end of each petal and glue on to the floral wire leaving around 2 to 3cm (0.8 to 1.2in) of the flower stamens showing. Glue the rest of the petals around the stamens, overlapping and pinching together to secure.

6 For the calyx, cut out a piece of the 180g red crepe paper measuring 3.5 x 5cm (1.4 x 2in). Stretch the paper out fully and cut out four pieces from the template. Apply a little glue to the straight, cut end and glue to the top of the petals, all four at 90 degrees to each other, sitting directly on top of the petals.

7 To make the coloured tube above the flower, cut a 5mm (0.2in) wide strip of the 180g red crepe paper and stretch the strip out fully.

8 Glue the strip directly below the four calyx on a 45-degree angle, pinch to secure and bring the strip down with a little glue about 1.5cm (0.6in). Then wrap back up the wire to the top again, tear and glue down the strip.

6

7–8

9 Next take a strip of 180g dark-green crepe paper 8cm x 4mm (3.1 x 0.2 in), stretch fully and wrap around with a light layer of glue directly underneath the tube to make an oval shape covering 6mm (0.24in) of the floral wire. This time focus mainly in the centre when you wrap, to create a small round shape. You can stop and tear off the strip and glue it down when the shape you've made looks in proportion.

10 Then wrap underneath this with a 5mm (0.20in) stretched strip of the 180g burgundy crepe paper, covering about 2.5cm (1in) of the stem wire. Then cut the wire stem to give a 20cm (8in) long flower, from the end of the stamen to the end of the wire. Repeat to make eight flowers in total.

12

To make a bud

11 We use the same technique with strips of paper to make a bud. Take a piece of 24-gauge paper-covered floral wire for each bud and create a thin long oval shape on the end of each separate wire with a 180g red crepe paper 5mm (0.2in) strip, adding more layers around the centre to make the oval shape. Keep adding a light layer of glue as you go. You can make three or four for your branch, ranging in size between 1 to 3cm (0.4 to 1.2in) in length. Then repeat a small oval of 180g dark-green crepe paper underneath, like we did with the flowers, and again cover 2cm (0.8in) of the stem with the burgundy paper.

12 Cut each bud stem down to 3cm (1.2in) for the smallest bud using the wire cutters, gradually increasing this to 15cm (6in) for the largest bud, in preparation for constructing the branch.

To make a leaf

13 I make around 15 leaves per branch, with a mix of the three different leaf sizes from the templates (three of the small leaf, five of the medium and seven of the large). These are all made in doublette crepe paper. To make the leaves we use a 26-gauge wire this time and cut the leaves on the bias as per the instructions on page 23. I then wrap around 1cm (0.40in) of a 5mm (0.20in) burgundy strip directly underneath the leaf to cover some of the floral wire.

14 Trim down each leaf wire with wire cutters to about 1.5cm (0.60in) below the end of the burgundy paper.

15 Add a little white pastel pencil to the bottom 1.5cm (0.60in) of each leaf to break up the green a little.

16 Flute the edges of the leaves gently between your fingers, following the instructions for this on page 18.

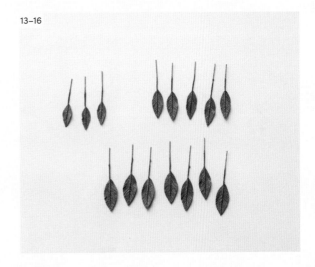

13–16

To assemble the branch

17 We will attach the buds first in order of size, along with the smallest leaves, then the flowers. Take a 5mm (0.2in) strip of the 180g burgundy crepe paper to begin with and add a light layer of glue at the top, smoothed over with your finger. Hold together two of the smallest leaves.

18 Wrap together at the same height and continue to wrap tightly around once or twice and add the smallest bud about 1cm (0.4in) down the stem. Bend the bud down, so you can see where to place the next items. It's good to create a gradual curve from the tip of the branch down to the end of the first flower. Wrap around the branch again and then add in the next small leaf, then wrap again and add the next bud, bending it downwards so it hangs at a lower height to the previous one. Add more glue when you can feel it has run out on the strip. Wrap tightly and try to keep the wires as straight as possible.

19 Continue to add leaves, buds and the flowers, moving through to the larger-sized leaves and buds as you go. If you need to change to a thicker branch strip of burgundy crepe paper to make sure all the wires are covered as they thicken, then do this. It's good to add two flowers together at some points, along with two leaves as close to the point where the flowers meet the branch as possible. You can vary the spacing between the flowers as you wish; I tend to leave a gap of between 2 to 3cm (0.8 to 1.2in) between each set of leaves and flowers.

20 Once all the items have been added, you can continue to wrap down the rest of the stem, adding in a piece of 18-gauge floral wire at this point to give you a long stem. Cut the wires with wire cutters at the point that you would like the branch to end. You can repeat the wrapping of the branch stem to give you a consistent thickness where needed.

21 You can now style the branch by bending the branch into a gentle curve, curling some of the calyxes on the flowers up with the end of your small scissors, bending some variety into the leaves and pulling some down towards the flowers.

18

20

Variegated tulip

The vibrant red stripes of this tulip really drew me in when I first saw it. We use collage to add the red detail, which takes a little time but is really satisfying to see come together and is really effective too. They can be styled with the petals pushed back or together.

You will need

180g Italian crepe paper in light
   yellow 574, yellow 17E5 and
   cream 577
60g Italian crepe paper in red 312
160g German florist crepe paper
   in grass green
Doublette crepe paper in olive/
   light olive
18-gauge floral wire
30-gauge white paper-covered
   floral wire
Conté pastel pencil in yellow 004
Standard scissors and precision
   scissors
Card, tracing paper and pencil
   for templates (see page 172)
Ruler
Aleene's Original Tacky Glue
Tweezers
Wire cutters

To make the centre

1 Take a piece of 18-gauge floral wire and a 5mm (0.2in) wide strip of 180g yellow crepe paper. Stretch the paper strip out fully and with a light layer of glue at the top, wrap around the top of the wire and down the top 2cm (0.8in) of the wire on a 45-degree angle. Wrap back up and down repeatedly until you have a 4mm (0.2in) thickness with the paper.

2 Wrap around the very top of the wire again repeatedly until this is built up thicker. Then add just one layer of paper at the base covering a further 1cm (0.4in) of the bare wire. Rip and glue down the strip at this point and then with a pair of tweezers, pinch three lines meeting in the very top to form the pistil.

3 To make six stamens, laminate a piece of 180g yellow crepe paper, stretched out and measuring 4 x 5cm (1.6 x 2in) in height, following the instructions on page 19. Then cut out the stamen template six times. Fold each stamen down the centre and bring to a point at the base.

4 Take each stamen and glue around the centre equally with the top of the stamen lining up with the top of the pistil.

To make the petals

5 We need six petals in total: three small and three large. Cut a stretched out piece of the 180g cream crepe paper on the bias for each petal and glue down as per the instructions for leaves on page 22. Cut out each of the petals from the templates with the fold going down the centre of the petal.

6 Add a 7cm (2.8in) piece of 30-gauge white paper-covered floral wire into the seam at the back of the petal and trim the seam down so it is tidy. Apply a light layer of glue to stick the seam down.

7 Take the petal in your fingers and very gently cup into the petal from the back, pushing the bottom of the petal out to a slight convex shape at the bottom.

8 To add the red detail to the petals, cut slivers of 60g red crepe paper, with a long thinly-cut sliver of crepe paper going down the centre of the petal from the top to the bottom. My tip would be to apply a light layer of glue where you think you will apply the slivers rather than adding it to the slivers. Apply to

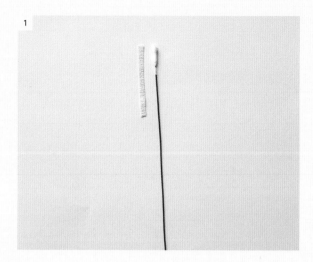

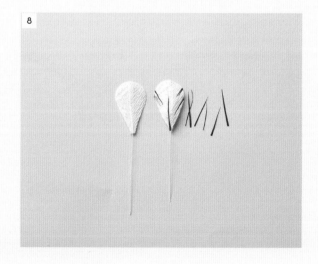

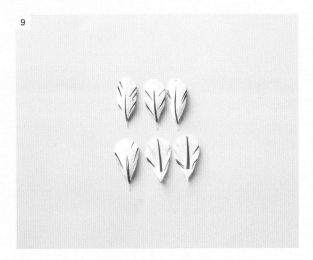

both sides of the petal, although on the internal side of the petal, leave a gap of 1cm (0.4in) clear of any red collage at the base of the petals. You can also make small, curved slivers and glue them to both or either side of the petal. Another tip would be to vary the placing of the markings a little on each side and petal. Repeat with the rest of the petals.

9 Once they are dry, fill in the bottom gap on the inside of the petal with thick yellow pastel and add a light amount of yellow pastel pencil to the outside of each petal.

10 Cut the white paper-covered floral wire down to 1cm (0.4in) below the base of the petal and apply a little glue to the wire. Wipe off the excess. Glue the three small petals on first equally around the centre, with the base of the petal sitting at the base of the stamen on the thin covering of paper. Then glue the three larger petals behind and in-between.

Leaves and stem

11 Cut the wire stem to the length that you require. If you would like to add a bulb, you can follow the instructions for this on pages 43–45, using a 2cm (0.8in) or larger polystyrene ball.

12 Take a stretched 1cm (0.4in) wide strip of 160g grass-green crepe paper and wrap around the stem, starting at the base of the white wires and following the instructions on page 20. Cut and glue at the end to secure. Repeat to get a thickness on the stem of about 3mm (0.1in), covering the white wires on the next wrap. Repeat again from whichever point is needed to obtain a consistent width of stem.

13 To make the leaves, cut one leaf from each of the two leaf templates using the olive/light olive doublette crepe paper. Apply a little glue to the base of each leaf and place these opposite each other on the stem around 5cm (2in) from the base, or more than that if the stem is very long. Gently curl them out a little with your fingers to give shape.

14 Now you can style your tulip; bend the stem to a gentle curve. Put a little pressure on the base of each petal inside the flower-head with your fingers, and if you do it to all the petals it will open up the size of the flower. You can also splay the petals fully open if you prefer.

Icelandic poppy

These lend themselves so well to being made in crepe paper as the petals are papery in real life. If you want to keep things simple you could make these in plain crepe papers rather than adding the colouring, although the colouring does bring something special to the flower. It's really satisfying and fun to create the pleats in the paper too.

You will need

180g Italian crepe paper for the stamen in light green 558 and yellow 17E5, and for the petals in cream 577, yellow 574 and orange 610

160g German florist crepe paper in grass green

8mm (0.3in) plastic bead

18-gauge floral wire

Dr. Ph. Martin's Hydrus Watercolors in hansa yellow light 1H for white poppies, chrome yellow 26H for yellow poppies and vermilion hue 27H for orange poppies.

Standard scissors and precision scissors

Card, tracing paper and pencil for templates (see page 170)

Ruler
Wire cutters
Aleene's Original Tacky Glue
Hot glue and glue gun
Watercolour paintbrush
Saucer/container for watercolours
Water and jar
Tweezers

To make a bud (optional)

1.5cm (0.6in) polystyrene ball

To make the stamen

1 Cut a rectangle of 180g light-green crepe paper across the grain measuring 7 x 5cm (2.8 x 2in). Stretch fully between your fingers.

2 Next, cut three strips of 180g yellow crepe paper across the grain, measuring 7cm x 5mm (2.8 x 0.2in) and stretch these between your fingers.

3 Apply glue all along the top edge of the green rectangle piece and smooth over the glue with your finger. Then press the stretched yellow piece down along the edge, covering the green. You need to cover the top edges on both sides of the green strip and then cover one side twice with two layers of yellow on top of one another. Firmly press the pieces together and set aside to dry.

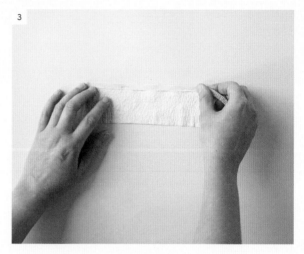

4 Next, hot glue an 8mm (0.3in) plastic bead to the top of a piece of 18-gauge floral wire. Then cut a piece of 160g grass-green crepe paper measuring 1 x 2cm (0.40 x 0.80in) and stretch between your fingers. Apply a light layer of glue across the paper, smooth with your finger and wrap around the bead to completely cover it.

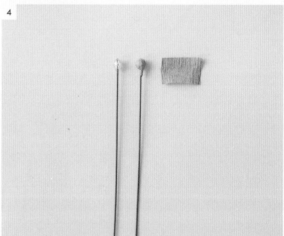

5 To make the lines across the centre of the plastic bead, cut a strip of 180g light-green crepe paper, this time cutting with the grain, measuring 20 x 3.5cm (8 x 1.4in). Stretch between your fingers and then cut a strip measuring 1cm (0.4in) wide, lengthways down the paper.

6 Apply a layer of glue down the right edge of the strip, spreading with your finger, and glue the strip in half lengthways then glue in half again. Finally, with clean hands, twist the piece into a thin strip with your fingers from the top down to the bottom.

7 To wrap the strip around the plastic bead, hold the strip at one end with one hand underneath the ball and wrap directly over the top of the ball, then holding the strip in place, wrap again to form a cross. Then secure underneath with a stretched 1cm (0.4in) strip piece of 160g grass-green crepe paper with a light layer of glue on it. Cut the light-green strip and then repeat this again in-between the lines of the cross to form a star shape.

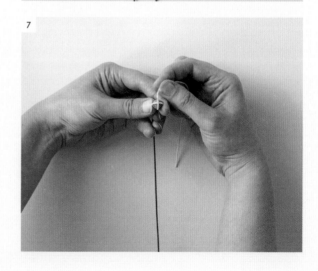

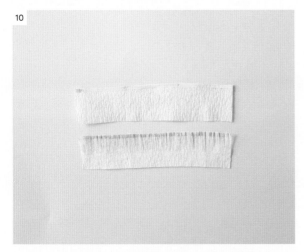

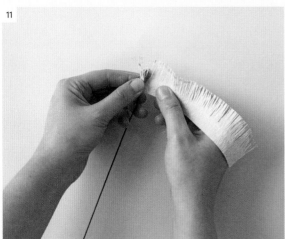

8 Once this is secure and while the papers are still damp from the glue, use a pair of tweezers to pinch together each strand of paper making up the centre and to give them all a uniform look.

9 Then wrap a strip of 160g grass-green crepe paper halfway round the plastic bead to cover the sides, being careful to make sure the top edge is fully glued down and not coming away at all.

10 Now we can go back to the green and yellow strip we prepared earlier (in step 3) and trim this down, cutting the width of the yellow piece at the top to 5mm (0.2in), the depth of the strip to 3cm (1.2in) and the length to 15cm (6in). Then fringe this piece as finely as you can (see instructions on page 18) 2cm (0.8in) of the way down the strip starting at the top with the yellow.

11 Next, apply a little glue to the bottom-left corner, smooth over with your finger and wrap this around the centre evenly with the bottom of the fringe sitting at the bottom of the plastic bead. Keep applying a little more glue as you go and smoothing it over, then secure at the end.

To make the petals

12 We need to cut two small petals and two large petals per flower. Cut two rectangles of 180g crepe paper in your choice of colour that fit the width and height of each petal template. Stretch each piece out fully between your fingers and cut out the templates.

13 Then take the watercolour that corresponds to the paper colour you've chosen and following the instructions on page 12, apply a gradual wash of colour over each petal..

14 Once dry we can add the pleats, referring to the instructions on page 19. Take one of the petals, stretch again and then rest on a smooth tabletop. Starting at one end, gather the edge of the petal against your thumbs, then when you reach the end, twist the gathered paper round on itself slightly. Repeat with each petal.

15 Apply a little glue again to the base of each petal and place the two small petals directly opposite each other and directly underneath the bottom of the fringed centre. Then add the two large petals in the same way, filling the two gaps on either side of the small petals. It does help the flower to look even if you try and keep the alignment of the petals as symmetrical as possible underneath the flower-head. Pinch all the paper firmly underneath to secure.

To make the stem

16 Cut down the wire stem with wire cutters to make your flower shorter if you prefer.

17 To cover the excess paper underneath the flower-head, take a 1cm (0.4in) wide strip of the 160g grass-green crepe paper, stretch between your fingers, apply a light scraping of glue to the end, smooth over with your finger and wrap in a parallel line underneath the flower, applying a little more glue as you go. Bring the strip down slightly to cover any paper lower down too.

18 Continue to wrap the stem with the same colour paper following the instructions on page 20. Wrap around four to five times to get the right thickness.

17

To make a bud

19 Hot glue a 1.5cm (0.6in) polystyrene ball to the end of a length of 18-gauge floral wire, making sure 5mm (0.2in) of the wire pierces the top. Take a 1cm (0.4in) strip of 160g grass-green crepe paper, apply a light layer of glue and wrap this around the polystyrene and the wire, building up the layers and adding more glue as you go until you have an oval shape. Take a 4 x 4cm (1.6 x 1.6in) piece of 160g grass-green crepe, stretch out and cut out four of the bud template. Cup each piece gently and apply glue over the bottom half of each piece. Then glue around the base of the bud shape, bringing them to a point at the top. Wrap the stem with a 1cm (0.4in) wide strip of the 160g grass-green crepe paper, covering around 16cm (6.2in) of the stem. Tear, glue down and repeat again to make it a little thicker. Then glue to the stem of your poppy, adding it at around 10cm (4in) from the bottom. Repeat with your wrapping if needed to get a consistent thickness on the stem.

20 You can now style the flower. Bring the flower-head forward and make the stem as bendy as you like to mirror the beautiful shapes of the poppy stems you see in real life. Then bend over the top of the bud and curve the stem.

19

Lisianthus

I first made these for a wedding commission and they became a really popular flower, partly due to their lovely delicate colouring. These look particularly great in a quantity, so it's really effective to make a bunch of them. You can change the position and number of flowers and buds on each stem to give lots of variety to your display.

You will need

180g Italian crepe paper in dark
   green 562, orange 610, pink 569
   and light green 558
60g Italian crepe paper in green
   264
20-gauge floral wire
24 and 26-gauge paper-covered
   floral wire
Sennelier soft pastels in peach 684
   and green 230
Standard scissors and precision
   scissors
Card, tracing paper and pencil
   for templates (see page 170)
Ruler
Wire cutters
Aleene's Original Tacky Glue
Scalpel
Pastel or cosmetic sponges and
   ceramic dish
Fine paintbrush

To make the stamen

1 Take a strip of 180g dark-green crepe paper 5mm (0.2in) wide, stretch between your fingers, apply a light layer of glue and pinch tightly over the top of a length of 20-gauge floral wire and bring it down on a 45-degree angle with a light layer of glue, covering the top 3cm (1.2in). Then wrap back up to the top and around the top a few times to make it larger at the very end, moulding the paper with your fingers. Apply a little more glue as you go.

2 Next, take a 3 x 3cm (1.2 x 1.2in) piece of 180g orange crepe paper, stretch this out fully and cut out a piece from this measuring 2 x 2.5cm (0.8 x 1in). Cut this piece with the grain into five fringed pieces, leaving the bottom 7mm (0.3in) intact. Take your precision scissors and cut the end of each strand into a curve. Then take each piece between your fingers and fold down the centre of each one with the nails of your thumb and forefinger. Add a light layer of glue to the bottom of the orange piece and place around the bottom of the green centre, ensuring the stamen strands are as evenly spaced as possible and sitting level with the top of the green. With the closed blades of your precision scissors and the top of your thumb, curve the top of the stamen heads in towards the green centre.

3 Then wrap another 5mm (0.2in) strip of 180g dark-green crepe paper tightly around the area at the bottom of the stamens with a light layer of glue, building up a small round ledge for the petals to sit on which measures approximately 5mm (0.2in) at the widest point.

1–3

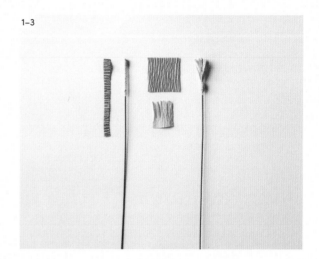

To make the petals

4 Cut a 12 x 5cm (4.7 x 2in) strip of 180g pink crepe paper. Stretch the paper between your fingers fully, then cut out six petals from the template which will make one flower.

5 To smooth each petal, hold the petal with both hands and with your thumb and forefinger drag your thumbnail down the surface of the top half of each petal to smooth the paper.

6 To add colour to each of the petals, apply a light amount of peach pastel to the top edge of the petal on both sides. Try to make sure there is a very subtle gradation of colour following the instructions on page 12.

7 To give shape to the petals, take each one and cup deeply (see page 19) in the bottom half, then scrape the top edge of each petal over the closed blades of your precision scissors. Flute each edge of the petals between your fingers (see page 18).

8 Apply a light layer of glue to the base of one petal. Place the second petal on top of the first, overlapping by two-thirds but gluing together at the bottom point of the petals. Continue doing this with the remaining petals until you have what looks like a small fan shape of petals. Apply glue to the bottom of this whole piece and wrap the left-hand side around the centre, with the bottom of the petals sitting at the bottom of the raised piece underneath the stamen. Wrap the fan of petals around in a swirl, keeping them at the same height so the top of the flower-head looks even. Add a little more glue if the petals aren't securing in place.

To make a bud

9 We need to make two buds, one a little smaller than the other. To make these, repeat the same method we used to make the green central stamen. Take a strip of 180g light-green crepe paper, stretch and apply a light layer of glue to the paper. Wrap around and gently over the top of a piece of 24-gauge paper-coverd floral wire. Then continue to wrap on a 45-degree angle, covering the top 2 to 2.5cm (0.8 to 1in) and back up, then down again, focusing on the bottom half, creating a tapered bud shape, with a round bottom and thinner towards the top, moulding and shaping with your fingers.

10 Cut a strip of the same stretched 180g light-green crepe paper, 6cm (2.4in) long and 8mm (0.31in) wide, fold in half lengthways, then trim the folded strip down to 4mm (0.2in) wide with your standard scissors.

11 Glue the folded strip down at the base of the bud on a 45-degree angle and with a light layer of glue, wrap around the bud in a spiral up to the top. Cut with scissors and glue down.

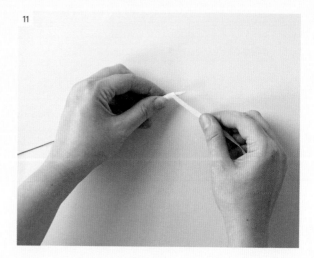

11

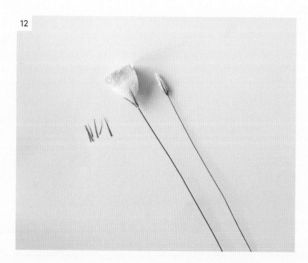

12

To make the stem and leaves

12 To make the calyx for the flower and the bud, laminate two pieces of 60g green crepe together (see page 19). Cut a 2 x 2cm (0.8 x 0.8in) square. Then cut five fine, tapered slivers of paper freehand from the top of the square to the bottom for each flower. For the buds, cut four slivers very finely indeed, long enough to cover around half of the bud you've made. Apply a little glue to the thickest end of each piece and apply these evenly around the flower-head and bud. They need to stick fully to the bud.

13 To wrap the stems, first cut 7mm (0.3in) wide strips of 60g green crepe paper against the grain. Stretch a strip between your fingers, apply a little glue to the end and wrap around the bottom of the flower-head and then down the stem on a 45-degree angle, adding a little glue as you go. Cover around 10cm (4in) of the stem, then cut and glue down and repeat again so the wire is covered twice. With the bud stems, repeat this but cover 7cm (2.8in) for the larger bud and 4cm (1.6in) for the smaller one.

14 Now you can prepare your leaves (see page 19 on how to laminate paper). Cut the first two sets of leaf templates using two sheets of the laminated 60g green crepe paper. The third and largest set of leaves need to have a 26-gauge paper-covered floral wire placed in the centre of the paper, following page 22 on how to make leaves on the bias.

15

16

To assemble the flower

15 Start with the largest bud and attach the smallest bud together with it at the point where both stem strips run out. Place your first set of leaves here, opposite each other, with a little glue. To keep it all in place, wrap a 7mm (0.3in) wide strip of the 60g green crepe paper and a little glue around underneath the leaves and down the stem, covering a further 6cm (2.4in) of the stem with paper. Cut at that point and glue down, then repeat so you thicken the stem a little more.

16 This now attaches to the main stem of the flower, again where the crepe runs out on the stem and again the next set of leaves go here too. Attach them as before, keeping the multiple wires tight together and as straight as possible. You can then wrap the stem again, enclosing all the wires together, for a further 4cm (1.6in).

17 The two largest leaves then get attached at this point, bent at a slight angle so the wires sit flush along the stem. Wrap with a 1cm (0.4in) strip at this point around underneath the leaves and down the stem. Cut the wires together at the point you would like the stem to end and then continue to wrap to the bottom. Repeat the wrapping a couple more times to make it thicker.

18 As a finishing touch, gently sponge green pastel on to the bottom of the flower-head and the buds. With a fine, short paintbrush, add a stronger layer of colouring at the very bottom so that the pastel blends well as a whole with the main stem. You can then shape the leaves into the position you like and shape the wires of the stem too. I tend to shape the stems slightly at each point where the leaves meet the stem.

Coral Charm peony

Of all the flowers I've made, the Coral Charm peony is by far the most popular. For this project, I've made their beautiful blousy petals with a delicate lightweight crepe paper, so it's best to take extra care when shaping the petals and use a light amount of glue. We use two slight variations of colour for the petals with a main colour and an accent colour.

You will need

180g Italian crepe paper in orange
  610, yellow 578, mustard 579 and
  pink 547
60g Italian crepe paper in peach
  200 and 201
Doublette crepe paper in olive/
  light olive and green tea/cypress
160g German florist crepe paper
  in grass green
18 and 20-gauge floral wire
24 and 26-gauge paper-covered
  floral wire
Standard scissors and precision
  scissors
Card, tracing paper and pencil
  for templates (see page 173)
Ruler
Wire cutters
Aleene's Original Tacky Glue

To make the centre carpels

1 Follow the instructions for making the central carpels in the Bowl of Beauty peony tutorial on page 82, but instead of making three carpels in total, make four, with an additional one on 20-gauge floral wire.

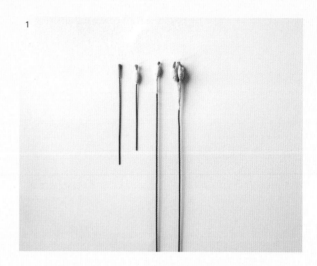

To make the stamens

2 Cut a rectangle of 180g orange crepe paper across the grain measuring 13 x 5cm (5 x 2in). Stretch fully between your fingers and cut out two pieces from the stamen template. Repeat again with the 180g yellow crepe paper and cut out one piece using the same template.

3 Take each piece and fold over, then finely fringe in the direction of the grain, down two-thirds of the length of the paper. The finer you fringe, the better the flower will look (see page 18).

4 Lay the three pieces down with the yellow piece in the centre and apply small dots of glue along the bottom uncut pieces to lightly secure the three pieces together. Twist the strands firmly together with your fingers to make the fringing even finer.

5 Then apply glue to the bottom-left corner, smooth across with your finger and wrap this around the carpels evenly, with the bottom of the fringe sitting at the bottom of the carpels. Keep applying a little more glue as you go, smoothing it over, then secure at the end. Push the paper together tightly underneath so it is completely secure.

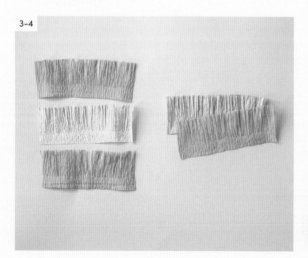

To make the petals

6 You can now choose which of the 60g peach crepe papers you would like to have as your main flower colour, with the other peach shade acting as the accent colour.

7 Cut out the petals from the 60g peach crepe paper of your choice using the templates. We need six of the small petals (four of the main colour and two of the lighter or darker accent colour), 30 of the large petals all cut from the main colour and one of the accent colours. You can accordion-fold the paper (see page 17) to make this quicker for you. At this stage, don't pay any attention to the dotted lines on the templates.

8 Cup the petals (see page 19) individually very gently between your thumb and fingers in the top third and then gently stretch underneath the curve you've created very slightly to straighten the petal. If you are creating harsh marks in the paper when you curve it, then you are applying too much pressure.

9 Cut detail into all the small petals and five of the large petals (including the accent-colour petal) following the dotted guidelines on the templates. Round off any straight cut edges that you make with precision scissors.

10 We can now apply the petals directly underneath the bottom of the fringed centre. Glue the small petals first, with a light layer of glue at the base. Place the first three small peach petals equally around the centre and then the next three in-between. Make sure you push each petal on firmly so that they don't start to come away from the centre.

11 Then work outwards with the detail-cut large petals first. Add the accent-colour petal so it almost forms a triangle with the other accent petals. Then add the next remaining petals by sight, keeping the flower as even as you can and filling any gaps in the petals from the previous layer of petals.

To make the calyx, leaves and stem

12 Follow the instructions on how to make the calyx, leaves and stem in the Bowl of Beauty peony tutorial on page 85. The only differences with this flower are that the leaves for this peony are made with doublette crepe paper instead of 160g green paper, but you can still wrap the stems with 160g grass-green florist crepe paper. You can see how to make leaves with doublette crepe paper on page 23.

13 You can then style the flower and bend the stem as you wish. I usually give the stem a little shape at each point that a leaf or flower comes off the main stem. You can also bring the flower-head down by gently pushing the wire forwards directly underneath the flower. Adjust any petals so they sit nicely and bring them out a little to fully open up the flower if you like.

Bowl of Beauty peony

I first saw this flower at the RHS Chelsea Flower Show, and I was immediately drawn to it. I adore the fluffy, unruly centre. The stamens can vary from yellow to cream and the petals from pink to lilac when they fade, so you could experiment with colours too.

You will need

180g Italian crepe paper in pink 547, mustard 579 and cream 603

Doublette crepe paper in lilac/light lilac and green tea/cypress

160g German florist crepe paper in grass green

60g Italian crepe paper in green 265

18 and 20-gauge floral wire

24 and 26-gauge paper-covered floral wire

Sennelier soft pastel in mustard 753

Standard scissors and precision scissors

Card, tracing paper and pencil for templates (see page 173)

Ruler

Wire cutters

Aleene's Original Tacky Glue

Scalpel

Pastel or cosmetic sponge and ceramic dish

To make the centre carpels

1 Cut a piece of the 180g pink crepe paper measuring 3 x 2cm (1.2 x 0.8in). Fully stretch out between your fingers and cut into 1cm (0.4in) wide pieces (we need three in total). Tear the top edges of each piece with your fingers to give a jagged edge. Apply a light layer of glue to each piece and roll firmly on to the end of one piece of 18-gauge wire and two pieces of 20-gauge wire, 3mm (0.10in) from the top of the paper.

2 Next, take thin 6mm (0.24in) wide strips of 180g mustard crepe paper, fully stretch out and apply a thin layer of glue to the first 5cm (2in). Starting at the top of the end of the wire, secure the paper at a 45-degree angle. Make a small oval shape with a larger centre, measuring around 5mm (0.2in) across at the widest point and 1.5cm (0.6in) long. Repeat with the other two wires too.

3 Cut each of the 20-gauge wires around 2cm (0.80in) from the bottom of each carpel and then push against each wire at the bottom of each to a 45-degree angle.

4 Take a thicker, stretched-out 1cm (0.4in) wide strip of 180g mustard crepe paper with a light layer of glue and place one of the shorter carpels level next to it. Wrap around tightly and add the next two carpels so all three sit closely together. Cut the strip and glue down once all the carpels are secure.

5 Push the three carpels firmly together.

1-3

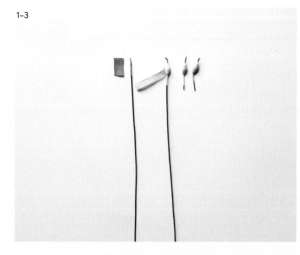

4-5

9

10

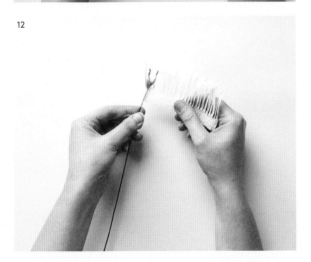

12

6 Stretch out a 13 x 7cm (5 x 2.8in) piece of 180g cream crepe paper fully and cut out the stamen centre template. You will need to cut out five of these altogether.

7 Take one piece and fold it over in half. Then cut lines freehand down the paper, leaving 1.5cm (0.6in) of the paper uncut at the bottom. Make the lines between 3 to 5mm (0.1 to 0.2in) apart.

8 Scrape the surface of the mustard pastel with a scalpel and carefully sponge pastel over the piece, close to the bottom of the cuts in the paper, creating a thin, subtle blend of colour (see page 12).

9 With your small precision scissors, cut out a deep triangle from the end of each strand. You can cut some a little higher so that each strand is not completely the same if you like.

10 Next, take the bottom of the first strand in your hands and using your thumbnail and forefinger, pinch the strand in half at the base of the cut and drag your thumbnail down the length of the strand. This will smooth the surface of the crepe paper and give some shape. Repeat this all the way along with each strand.

11 Repeat again with the remaining four pieces.

12 To attach these to the carpels, take a strip, apply a light layer of glue to the bottom left of the piece with the pastel facing you and place the bottom of the strands directly underneath the base of the carpels. With your right hand, pull the paper tightly and with your left hand turn the wire anticlockwise (keeping your hands close together). Keep applying glue now and then, smoothing it over with your fingers as you wrap. Once one piece is glued on, start again with the next strip until they are all glued around the centre. Push the paper together tightly underneath so it is completely secure.

To make the petals

13 Take a piece of lilac doublette crepe paper and cut out three petals from template 1, three petals from template 2, two petals from template 3 and three petals from template 4.

14 Gently cup each petal deeply in the centre on the light-lilac side of the paper (see page 19). On each petal, gather a small pleat in the bottom third of the petal to bring the base of the petal to a point. Apply a thin layer of glue down a little of the pleat at the front and back of the petal to secure.

15 Then apply another small amount of glue to the pointed base and glue the first three petals from template 1 directly underneath the stamens at even spaces around the centre. You can then add the petals from template 2. The first two petals can be placed halfway behind two of the first petals and the third can be placed in-between. From this point, you can add the remaining petals by sight, adding petals from template 4 last. Make sure to position them all level underneath the flower-head. Push the petal bases firmly together underneath the flower when each petal is applied so they are all secure.

15

15

16

20-21

To make the calyx, leaves and stem

16 To make the calyx, take a piece of the green-tea doublette crepe paper and cut three of each of the calyx pieces. Cup each of these in the centre to give shape and apply a light layer of glue to the bottom of each one. Glue the three small round pieces evenly directly underneath the centre and then place the three longer calyxes in-between.

17 To cover the base of the petals and the calyx, stretch a 1cm (0.4in) wide strip of 160g grass-green crepe paper and glue tightly around covering the base of the petals underneath the flower-head. Then bring this down on a 45-degree angle, applying a little glue as you go and continue down the wire stem, following the instructions on wrapping a stem on page 20. You can cut the length of the stem with wire cutters as well if you prefer a shorter flower. Wrap the stem tightly four or five times.

18 To make the leaves, trace and cut out the four leaf templates. Cut squares of 160g grass-green crepe paper on the bias (stretched out a little) for one of leaf template 1 and two each of the remaining three leaf templates: 2, 3 and 4. Follow the instructions on page 22 for making leaves on the bias. Then cut each of the individual leaves out.

19 Take a 15cm (6in) piece of 24-gauge paper-covered floral wire and lay this in the inside of the valley at the back of the template leaf 1 and two of template leaf 3. For the remaining leaves, place a length of 15cm (6in), 26-gauge paper-covered floral wire in the valley at the back of each. Press down along the back of each leaf firmly to secure. Cut the base of the leaf to a point with precision scissors so it fits nicely against the wire.

20 To assemble a leaf sprig, take the template 1 leaf and a stretched 6mm (0.24in) wide strip of the 60g olive-green crepe paper. See the instructions on page 24 on how to put a leaf sprig together. Wrap around at the base of the leaf for 1cm (0.4in). Take two of the template 2 leaves and place the leaves on each side at the base of the main leaf. Wrap all three leaves tightly together for about 3cm (1.2in). Tear the strip off and glue down.

21 Next prepare a smaller sprig to attach to this leaf. Take one of the template 3 leaves and another 6mm (0.24 in) wide strip of the 60g olive-green crepe paper, wrap in the same way as before, adding a template 4 leaf at the 1cm (0.4in) point. Wrap for just over another 1cm (0.4in) and then join to the first sprig. Wrap all the wires together for 1cm (0.4in) and then use the wire cutters to trim away the excess wire, staggering the length of the wires so they gradually reduce to just one wire that is longer. Repeat with the second leaf sprig (which has only two leaves joined together to give variety).

22 To attach the leaves to the main stem (see page 25) I place one leaf sprig about 9cm (3.5in) from the base of the flower and then a second sprig 1cm (0.4in) lower. I continue wrapping to ensure the stem looks even. You can wrap the stem again a couple of times from underneath the small leaf to the end of the stem, to make it thicker and consistent with the rest of the stem.

23 You can now style the flower and bend the stem as you wish. I usually give the stem a little shape at each point that a leaf or flower comes off the main stem. You can also bring the flower-head down by gently pushing the wire forwards, directly underneath the flower. Adjust any petals so they sit nicely.

Dahlia Café au Lait

This is a variety of dahlia called Dinner Plate dahlia and is one of the largest flowers in the book, with the flower-head being around 14cm (5.5in) in diameter. Its large, creamy petals make it a really elegant, impressive flower. I would recommend attempting this when you're feeling confident with your making as there are lots of petals to make and attach.

You will need

180g Italian crepe paper in cream 577, light green 558 and dark green 17A8
160g German florist crepe paper in grass green
1.5cm (0.6in) polystyrene balls
18-gauge floral wire
24 and 26-gauge paper-covered floral wire
Sennelier soft pastel in magenta 940
Standard scissors and precision scissors
Card, tracing paper and pencil for templates (see page 175)
Ruler
Wire cutters
Hot glue and glue gun
Aleene's Original Tacky Glue
Scalpel and ceramic dish for pastel
Pastel or cosmetic sponge

To make the centre

1 To make a base for the petals, skewer 3 x 1.5cm (0.6in) polystyrene balls on to a piece of 18-gauge floral wire, ensuring the wire doesn't push through the top ball, using hot glue to secure all three pieces.

2 Next, take a 1cm (0.4in) wide strip of 180g cream crepe paper, apply a thin layer of glue and wrap this continuously round the gaps in the polystyrene to even the surface. You can also wrap over the top to completely cover the polystyrene with paper.

3 Scrape a scalpel blade over the surface of the magenta pastel into a bowl and with a sponge apply some of this over the top of the polystyrene.

4 To prepare the small centre petals, take an 8 x 5cm (3 x 2in) piece of 180g cream crepe paper and stretch out fully. Fold over in half and laminate together, using the instructions on page 19. Cut out the centre template using this as a guide with precision scissors to cut out the details all the way along the strip, moving the template along as you go.

5 Apply a layer of magenta pastel to the strip of petals on the lower half (see page 12). Then take each petal on the strip in between your thumb and forefinger and fold a crease with your thumbnail down the centre of each petal. Then on the other side, apply a layer of glue over the uncut piece at the bottom. Wrap around the centre, at the point that will result in the top of the petals meeting in the centre of the polystyrene when pushed in towards each other. Apply a little glue to the polystyrene centre to secure the inner-most petals and ensure they almost meet together in the centre.

6 Repeat again with a second piece, this time measuring 4 x 5cm (1.6 x 2in), making sure to wrap again at the same point. The petals of the centre should curve towards each other in the centre and the outer petals should gradually stand vertical around the edge.

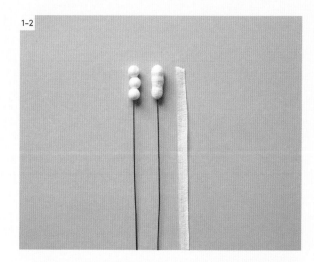

1–2

5

To prepare the petals

7 We need to cut out the following numbers of petals, from stretched-out 180g cream crepe paper. Petal 1 should be made with laminated 180g cream crepe paper. Cup each petal in the centre and then add magenta pastel lightly as follows:

Five x petal 1
(shade whole petals
with light layer of pastel)
Two x petal 2
(shade bottom two-
thirds of each lightly)
Three x petal 3
(shade bottom two-
thirds of each lightly)
Three x petal 4
(shade bottom half of
each lightly)

Six x petal 5
(shade bottom half
of each lightly)
Five x petal 6
(shade bottom half
of each lightly)
Six x petal 7
(shade bottom third
of each lightly)
42 x petal 8
(shade bottom third
of each lightly)

8 After adding pastel to each petal, add a little glue to the base and then bring to a point at the base, twisting slightly with your fingers. Then push down on the point to make it as flat as possible. Hold the petal between your forefinger and thumb and scrape the surface of the petal with your thumbnail to smooth and give some shape.

To add the petals

9 We'll work from the smallest petals first. Add a small amount of glue to the base of all the five smallest petals and glue these around the centre, almost evenly, so that the top of the glued base sits at the base of the 'teeth' of the central rolled petals. Then add the next two sets of petals in the same way, keeping them as level as possible at the base, but try not to make things too symmetrical.

10 Move on to the next size and when the petals are spaced evenly all around the centre, start on the second line of petals. Add this layer directly in-between the petals before, but 2 to 3mm (0.08 to 0.10in) lower down. The flower will look best if you attach the petal base by pushing it down firmly and ensure the petal sits in-between the previous petals throughout making the whole flower. It's also important that the petals sit in-between the petals on the layer above.

11 Continue to add the rest of the petals by sight in this way, dropping the next layer again 2 to 3mm (0.08 to 0.1in) lower, applying the bases of the petals level and so that the petals sit in-between, and the flower looks even. When you get to some of the largest petals, it can be easier to work holding the flower-head upside down. You can see more clearly where to add the remaining petals from the gaps in the petals bases too. Once all the petals are attached, the flower should be nice and full. The bottom layer of petals should be curved downwards over the blades of your scissors so that they start to droop slightly away from the flower.

To make the calyx and stem

12 To strengthen the stem, push two more 18-gauge floral wires into the polystyrene base alongside the wire already inserted and hot glue them into place.

13 To make the calyx, take a 6 x 3cm (2.4 x 1.2in) piece of the 180g light-green crepe paper, stretch out fully and cut out nine pieces from the template. Apply a little glue to the base of each calyx piece and glue around so that the base of each one sits on the bump of excess paper underneath the flower-head. Then cut 9 of the calyx template 2 from stretched out 180g green crepe and glue these in-between the previous layer of calyx pieces

14 Take a 1cm (0.4in) wide strip of the 160g grass-green crepe paper and with a light layer of glue, wrap this closely around the top of the bump to cover the base of the calyx pieces, then continue wrapping down to completely cover the bump with green.

15 With a stretched-out 1cm (0.4in) wide strip of 160g grass-green crepe paper, wrap the whole stem four times, following the instructions on page 20.

To make the leaves and assemble

16 Make the leaves from 180g dark-green crepe paper, cutting them on the bias following the instructions on page 22. In total we need to make two x leaf 2 and three each of the other leaves. With a 5mm (0.2in) wide strip of stretched 160g grass-green crepe paper, wrap underneath the base of each leaf by 2cm (0.8in).

17 Make two main leaf sprigs with three leaves each: one of each leaf template. Then make a third small stem with leaves 2 and 3 on only. Place the central leaf on each sprig on 24-gauge paper-covered wires and the remaining leaves on 26-gauge. Wrap with an 8mm (0.3in) strip of 160g grass-green crepe paper, with the lower leaves sitting 1 to 1.5cm (0.2–0.6in) below the central leaf. Of the two main sprigs, wrap one with a 3cm (1.2in) stem below the lower leaves and the other with a 6cm (2.4in) stem. With the smaller sprig, wrap down to 10cm (4in) below the leaves to give a long stem and wrap this twice to strengthen. Bend the stems at the end of

the paper and cut the sprig wires down individually and staggered so that they don't all stop in the same place. Apply a little glue to the point on the main stem where the leaves will be placed 16cm (6.2in) below the calyx and wrap around with a 1cm (0.4in) strip of the 180g dark-green crepe paper to secure all the three leaf stems at the same point.

18 Continue to wrap down the stem to cover the wires and wrap again if needed to hide any bumps on the stem and keep it a consistent thickness.

19 You can now style the flower. Bring the flower-head forward, gently bend the stem as you wish and adjust any leaves as needed. Once the glue for the petals is dry, you can pinch the ends of the petals together with your fingernails to give them shape and adjust them to make sure they sit in-between the petals on the previous layer.

Semi-cactus dahlia

These are dramatic flowers, with their star-like spikiness. The petals are wider at the base and then curl in on themselves and this is what makes them look spiky. It's quite satisfying to roll the shape into each petal.

You will need

180g Italian crepe paper in your choice of colour for the petals: orange 610, yellow 575 or purple 590 and green 17A8 for the leaves

160g German florist crepe paper in grass green

1.5cm (0.6in) polystyrene balls

18-gauge floral wire

24 and 26-gauge paper-covered floral wire

Short piece of 3mm (0.1in)-thick armature or floral wire (or other similar-shaped object)

Conté pastel pencil in medium yellow 004 for the orange and yellow flowers and Persian violet 055 for the purple flower (optional)

Standard scissors and precision scissors

Card, tracing paper and pencil for templates (see page 174)

Ruler

Wire cutters

Hot glue and glue gun

Aleene's Original Tacky Glue

To make the centre

1 To make a base for the petals, skewer 3 x 1.5cm (0.60in) polystyrene balls on to a piece of 18-gauge floral wire, ensuring the top one doesn't pierce all the way through the polystyrene. Hot glue the pieces in place, adding hot glue in-between and at the base.

2 Next, take a 1cm (0.4in) wide strip of the 180g crepe paper of your choice, apply a thin layer of glue and wrap this continuously around the polystyrene, focusing more on the in-between gaps to even out and cover the surface.

3 To prepare the small centre petals, take a 9 x 5cm (3.5 x 2in) piece of the same crepe paper and stretch out fully. Fold over in half and laminate together using the instructions on page 19. Cut out the centre template finely and use this as a guide to cut out a continuous strip of triangular 'teeth' rounded off slightly at the top using precision scissors and cut 1.5cm (0.6in) deep. The strip should be 20cm (8in) long.

4 Apply a light layer of glue to the base of the strip and wrap the piece around the top of the polystyrene, making sure the top of the teeth meet in the centre and form a small bud shape.

1–2

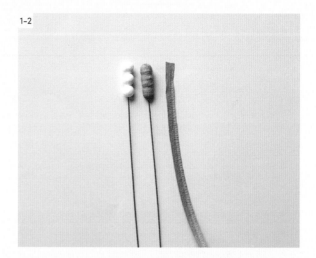

4

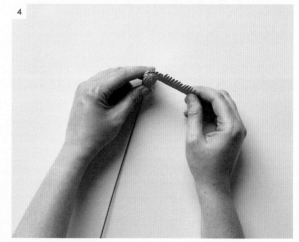

6

8

12

To add the petals

5 To make sure the petals keep a strong spiky shape, laminate two pieces of the paper together before cutting out each set of petals (see page 19). I prefer to work with the paper when it is still malleable from the glue, and it hasn't quite dried yet.

6 For the first set of petals, cut out six of petal 1 from the template in the laminated paper. Take each petal, and with a small length of 18-gauge wire, slightly curl over the top edges of the petal. Glue the six petals evenly around the centre with a light layer of glue. Place them at the base of the 'teeth' of the petals of the centre.

7 With the second set of petals, cut out six of these again. Take a small piece of the thick armature wire and shape the top two-thirds of the pointed shape around the wire, stretching ever so slightly so it takes on the rounded shape of the wire. This is how we shape all the rest of the petals from now on.

8 Apply a little glue to the base of the petals and place these in-between the first set of petals at the same height. From now on, bring the end of each petal to a slight point with your fingers.

9 For the third set of petals, cut out 12 of these and shape them in the same way. Glue these so that the first six sit behind the first set of petals, but 2mm (0.08in) lower than the previous line of petals. The remaining six of this size will sit in-between the petals you've just added.

10 For the fourth set of petals, cut out 12 of these for the next layer. Add these in-between the gaps of the layer before, but again bring this layer down 2mm (0.08in) from the previous.

11 We need to cut out, shape and add a further 33 petals of this size, continuing to add these in the same way, placing them in gaps in-between the petals of the previous layer. Each layer needs to be 2mm (0.08in) lower than the previous.

12 Cut 24 of the final petal template – these can be shaped and placed around the bottom of the layers as before. You may need to add more petals to ensure only around 1cm (0.4in) of the polystyrene base can be seen. Set the flower aside to dry.

To make the calyx and stem:

13 To make the calyx, take a 6 x 3cm (2.4 x 1.2in) piece of the 160g grass-green crepe paper, stretch out fully and cut out seven pieces from the template. Apply a little glue to the base of each calyx piece and glue around so that the base of each sits on the bump of excess paper underneath the flower-head. Take a 1cm (0.4in) wide strip of the 160g grass-green crepe paper and with a light layer of glue, wrap this closely around the top of the bump to cover the base of the calyx pieces, then continue wrapping down to completely cover the bump with green.

14 With a stretched-out 1cm (0.4in) wide strip of 160g grass-green crepe paper, wrap the whole stem a few times, until it reaches a thickness of about 3mm (0.1in).

15 Now we can move on to making the leaves, which are made in the same way as for the Dahlia tutorial on page 93, using the three sizes of templates. Make three sprigs of leaves, two large and one small with three leaves each on the larger sprigs and two on the long, small sprig. With this Dahlia the two main

sprigs are shorter, with 1–1.5cm distance between the main leaves and the lower leaves. They are then wrapped for 2–2.5cm down the leaf stem.

16 Apply a little glue to the point on the main stem where the smallest leaves will be placed 6.5cm (2.6in) below the calyx and wrap around with a 1cm (0.4in) strip of the 160g grass green crepe paper to secure.

17 Wrap the stem to the bottom and repeat again if needed to hide any bumps and ensure a consistent thickness.

18 You can now style the flower by gently shaping the lower petals of the flower downwards and creating the roundest shape possible for the whole flower. You can tilt the flower-head forwards a little, bend the stem as you wish and adjust the leaves so they have some variety.

19 As an optional finishing touch, you can apply a little pastel pencil to the centre of the base of some of the smallest petals, blending out with your finger if needed. This gives a little depth to the centre of the flower.

13

16

Lily regale

These are one of the most popular varieties of lily and it's not hard to see why, with the striking contrast of their pink outer stripes. Mixing the pastel colours together by hand can result in lovely natural colour variations. You can make them as tall as you like; with a very long stem of leaves they can look spectacular.

You will need

180g Italian crepe paper in light green 558

60g Italian crepe paper in orange 294

Doublette crepe paper in white and olive/light olive

160g German florist crepe paper in grass green

18 and 20-gauge floral wire

26-gauge paper-covered floral wire

30-gauge white paper-covered floral wire

Derwent Inktense pastel pencil in maroon 170

Sennelier soft pastels in pink 940, magenta 327, red 269 and yellow 098

Standard scissors and precision scissors

Card, tracing paper and pencil for templates (see page 171)

Ruler

Wire cutters

Aleene's Original Tacky Glue

Scalpel and 3 ceramic dishes

Pastel or cosmetic sponges

To make the centre

1 To make the central pistil, take a 20-gauge piece of floral wire and a 5mm (0.2in) strip of 180g light-green crepe paper. Stretch the strip fully between your fingers. Apply a light layer of glue to the end and wrap over the top of the wire, then bring it down to wrap the top 11cm (4.3in) of the wire. Tear the strip at this point and glue down. Then apply another light amount of glue to the strip again and this time wrap around the top of the wire a few times, shaping with your finger to create a small round shape at the end. Tear the strip again and glue down.

2 To make the six stamens, cut six wires of 26-gauge paper-covered floral wire, measuring approximately 18cm (7.in) each. Then take a strip of 60g orange crepe paper 5mm (0.2in) thick, stretch fully between your fingers, apply a light layer of glue to the end and pinch tightly over the top of a piece of the floral wire. Bring it down on a 45-degree angle, covering the top 1.5cm (0.6in). Then wrap back up to the top and around the centre again and again to make an oval shape, moulding the paper with your fingers. Apply a little more glue as you go. The oval should be 3mm (0.1in) wide across the centre point. Repeat this with all six wires. Then take a 5mm (0.20in) thick strip of the 180g light-green crepe paper and cover 10cm (4in) of the wire stem below the orange. You can then tear the strip and glue down.

3 To secure all these together, take a 1cm (0.4in) wide strip of the 180g light-green crepe paper, apply a light layer of glue to the end and place around the main carpel wire 11cm (4.3in) from the end. Take one of the stamens and line this up so that the orange tip lies around 1cm (0.4in) lower than the end of the carpel. Secure this with a little glue and wrap the strip over it to keep it in place. Then add a second stamen in the same way, level with the previous. You don't want things to get too bulky, so wrap tightly and place the others in one by one now, keeping all at the same level as you wrap around, securing each with glue. Once all the stamens are secured, cut each of the slim 26-gauge wires with wire cutters and cover the ends with the strip of paper. You can bend them together into a very shallow curve down the full length of the stamen.

3

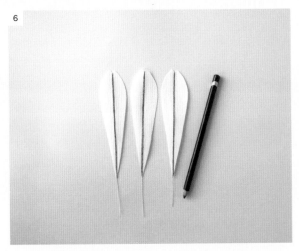

To make the petals

4 Cut six petals in total for each full bloom from white doublette crepe paper, three each of petal templates 1 and 2, with the grain running down the length of each petal. With the three larger petals, (petal template 2) fold in half lengthways. Then apply a thin trail of glue inside the crease line from the top to the bottom. Take an 18cm (7in) piece of 30-gauge white paper-covered floral wire and place into the line of glue from the top to the bottom of the petal. Smoothly run over the wire with your finger to secure and wipe off any excess glue. Let it dry and repeat this with the other two larger petals.

5 Once dry, turn each petal over to the plain side, lay horizontal and feel the line of the wire along the petal. Pinch the wire with your thumb and forefinger through the paper and drag your fingernails along the wire to make an impression of it through the paper. Repeat again with the other two petals.

6 Take the Derwent pastel pencil and, with the point, draw a slim but solid line down the raised paper impression of the wire. The wire should sit on the other side of the paper. Fold the petal over along the wire line and carefully draw each edge and side of the wire down the centre of the petal. You want the colour to look continuous and neat. You can blend very carefully with your finger if you need to smooth the colour. Repeat with the other larger petals.

7 For the three smaller petals (petal template 1), we need to add colour first. See page 12 on how to add pastel to paper. With a pastel sponge, add a little pastel to the petal, forming a light layer of pink down the centre of the petal but not quite covering to the edges. Then take the magenta and red pastels and file down equal amounts of these two colours together into a dish. With a second pastel sponge, add this colour down the centre of the petal, blending evenly. You can then repeat the impression of the wire from the previous petals on to the coloured side of this petal, using your fingernails to bring this through. Then add a line of colour down the wire impression with your pastel pencil the same as before. Repeat with the other two petals.

8 To prepare the petals before we place them together, cut the base of each petal to a point, trimming away the excess paper.

9 Then to join them all together, we need to place the petals together in a fan shape, alternating between a petal 1 and a petal 2. Start with a petal 1 on the wired side and apply a line of glue on the bottom-right edge of the petal up to the centre point of the edge. Lay a petal 2 on top, placing the left bottom edge directly next to the centre wire of petal 1. Then place a second petal 1 underneath the right edge, this time applying a line of glue down the bottom left-hand edge. You need this to be repeated until all the petals are glued together in a fan shape; glued at the same point across all the pieces. Make sure the centre lines on each petal on the other side aren't covered.

10 Referring to the pastel instructions on page 12, add a gradation of yellow pastel over the bottom 5cm (2in).

11 Then take the far left and right of the fan of petals and join those two edges together, ensuring the petals are glued together in the same way. You should now have the lily trumpet shape. Push out the edges of the petals with a gentle curve and lightly flute the edges following the instructions on page 18.

12 Next you can place the centre pieces through the top of the trumpet so they are around 1 to 2cm (0.4 to 0.8in) from the top of the petals. Gather the white wires to a point at the base of the lily. Cut a 1cm (0.40in) wide strip of the 160g grass-green crepe paper and with a light layer of glue on the strip, wrap this around at the point the wires meet to secure them in place. Then cut the wires with wire cutters around 1cm (0.4in) from this point to reduce bulk on the stem. Continue to wrap the strip around to cover the end of the wires. If this point seems a little bumpy, wrap a little more with the strip to ensure that the surface is as smooth as possible. Wrap to around 6cm (2.4in) and then tear the strip and glue down. Repeat if you'd like to make another flower for your lily stem.

13

To make a bud

13 We use the same principal to make a bud, although this time the petals are all the same size and there are four instead of five. Cut the petals using the bud template. Wire each petal as before and apply the same colouring as petal 1 to all the petals. Glue them together as before and gather the base around the end of a piece of 20-gauge floral wire wrapped with a little paper (I don't include stamens in the bud) and then cut the white wires and wrap as before.

To make the leaves and stem

14 To add a little leaf to each of the flowers, stretch a piece of 160g grass-green crepe paper and cut freehand a couple of tapered leaves measuring around 3 to 4cm (1.2 to 1.6in) in length. Add a little glue to the base and glue 2.5 to 3cm (1 to 1.2in) from the base of the flower-heads. You can create a bend in the leaves by curling them very slightly over the closed blades of your precision scissors.

15 Take a 1cm (0.40in) wide strip of 160g grass-green crepe paper and apply a light layer of glue to the end. Place the stem of the bud and a flower together, positioning the bud higher, joining them 3cm (1.2in) from the base of the bud and 5.5cm (2.2in) from the base of the flower. At this point where they meet on the stem, I add in a piece of 18-gauge floral wire with the strip to strengthen the stem and I hide the bump on the stem from this by placing a leaf over it. We can add more leaves and wrap these into the strip of green crepe paper. Add around five leaves again, cut freehand and curled as above from the 160g grass-green crepe paper, varying in length from 3 to 5cm (1.2 to 2in).

15

16 Continue wrapping down the stem and add in a second flower if you like, around 2 to 3cm (0.8 to 1.2cm) below the others. I bend the stem slightly at the point it will join, apply a little glue to the stem of the flower and then wrap around to secure with a strip before continuing to wrap down the stem.

17 At this point, with the floral wire for each part being at different lengths, we will wrap the rest of the stem and make sure we keep the thickness of the stem uniform. As you meet the end of a piece of floral wire, add another at the end to keep the stem the same thickness throughout. I finish with a stem around 40cm (16in) long and cut it down to this length with wire cutters. I then go back to the top when I have finished and repeat the wrap five or six times to thicken the stem.

18 Now you can prepare your main leaves. Cut these from olive/light olive doublette crepe paper with the grain running lengthways. Cut five of the first leaf template and eight of the second. The leaves run down the stem, in clusters of two to three leaves evenly placed around the stem. Add the first two leaves with a little glue at the base around 5cm (2in) from where the lower flower joins. Place them directly opposite each other. Use a stretched 1cm (0.40in) piece of the 160g grass-green crepe paper to wrap around and cover the base of the leaves. Tear the paper and glue down once one wrap has been done. Repeat down the stem at irregular intervals, placing three leaves evenly around the stem at some places and two leaves at others.

19 As a finishing touch, gently apply a little of the maroon pastel pencil to the point where each flower-head meets the green stem so that it blends seamlessly. You can point the bud and flower-heads up and style the leaves so they don't look too uniform.

16–17

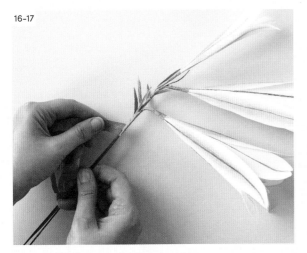

18

Cupcake cosmos

A flower with a wonderful name, to match my favourite variety of cosmos. The leaves are very fine so they take a little time but are well worth it.

You will need

180g Italian crepe paper in yellow 576, brown 568 and pink 17A3
Doublette crepe paper in olive/ light olive
160g German florist crepe paper in grass green
18-gauge floral wire
24-gauge paper-covered floral wire
Sennelier soft pastel in magenta 940
Standard scissors and precision scissors
Card, tracing paper and pencil for templates (see page 171)
Ruler
Wire cutters
Aleene's Original Tacky Glue
Scalpel
Pastel or cosmetic sponge

To make the centre

1 Cut a piece of the 180g yellow crepe paper 12 x 2cm (4.7in x 0.8in), stretch out and fold over lengthways and then fold again. Finely fringe 5mm (0.2in) all the way along the bottom edge with precision scissors.

2 Roll the strands together firmly with dampened fingers to create even finer strands of paper.

3 Repeat these two steps with the 180g brown crepe paper, but this time cut down to 1.5cm (0.6in) width. If the brown paper stretches further than the yellow when fully stretched out, cut down to match the length of the yellow piece.

4 Glue down the brown strip 2mm (0.08in) from the top of the yellow fringed piece.

5 Cut away a diagonal slanted piece from the bottom of the halfway point to just below the fringe at the right-hand end of the strip. This will reduce bulk at the back of the flower.

6 Wrap tightly around the top of a length of the 18-gauge wire, pulling the strip tightly with one hand and rolling the strip around the wire with the other. Bring down the strip 1 or 2mm (0.04 or 0.08in) around the halfway point to form a very slight, gradual dome to the tightly-wrapped paper.

7 Press firmly together to secure in place.

1-5

6

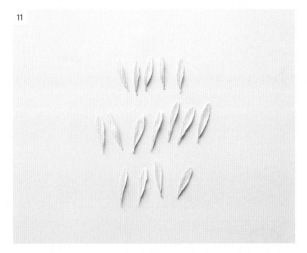

11

12

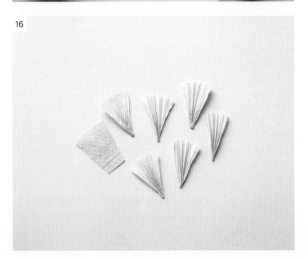

16

To make the inner petals

8 Stretch out a 10 x 6cm (4 x 2.4in) strip of 180g pink crepe paper fully and cut out five petals from each of the templates 1, 2 and 3.

9 Hold each paper petal individually in your hand and scrape down your thumbnail over the surface to smooth (see page 18 on removing grain).

10 Carefully sponge magenta pastel over the bottom third of each petal, giving the paper a gentle gradation of colour (see page 12).

11 Add a light layer of glue on the bottom edge of each petal, pinch together right at the bottom and roll between your fingers to a point.

12 Apply another small amount of glue to the gathered end of the petals and place the petals directly underneath the fringe of the centre, although not on the fringe itself. Start with the smallest petals first and add, by sight, evenly around the centre. Work up to the largest size, adding these behind, filling gaps, and leaving a little space here and there so that it looks natural. Make sure to keep the ends of the petals level underneath the flower so they are all attached at the same height. Firmly pinch underneath the centre fringe when each petal is applied to ensure it stays in place.

To make the outer petals

13 Take another 20 x 8cm (8 x 3in) strip of 180g pink crepe paper, stretch out fully and cut six outer petals using the template.

14 As with the inner petals, scrape with your thumbnail down the whole of each cut-petal paper to smooth the grain.

15 Apply a light amount of magenta pastel carefully all over the lower half of each petal, making sure there is a subtle gradation of colour.

16 Place pleats into each petal, following the instructions on page 19. Use your fingernails again to scrape along the length of the petal, creasing the lines firmly into the paper.

17 Pinch together the paper on the glued edge to form a point and secure the paper together.

18 Use the pleated lines as a guide to cut in the jagged edges of the petals with precision scissors, making the points of the edges lie at the point of a pleat. Cut them around 3mm (0.1in) deep, making some slightly larger and some smaller to give variation.

19

20

19 Glue each petal 2mm (0.08in) underneath the inner petals. Place side-by-side and at the same height, gluing the right edge of the first petal to the left edge of the second. Continue all the way around until each petal is glued on to the next.

To make the calyx, leaves and stem

20 Cut a piece of the olive/light olive doublette crepe paper measuring 2 x 3cm (0.8 x 1.2in) and cut out eight thin triangles from the top edge to the bottom. Apply a small dot of glue to the wider bottom edge of each triangle and place equally around the underneath of the base of the flower-head.

21 To cover the base of the petals and the calyx, stretch a 1cm (0.4in) wide strip of 160g grass-green crepe paper and glue around the base of the petals, pressing it tightly around the underneath of the flower-head. Then bring this down on a 45-degree angle, applying a little glue as you go and continue down the stem, following the instructions on wrapping a stem on page 20. You can cut the length of the stem with wire cutters as well if you like. I wrap the stem tightly three times.

To make foliage

22 Take another piece of olive/light olive doublette crepe paper, this one measuring 5 x 5cm (2 x 2in). Cut long and thin triangles down the length of the paper, about 3 to 4mm (0.1 to 0.2in) wide at the base. I make around 12 or 13 per leaf.

23 To put the leaf together, take an 18cm (7.1in) piece of 24-gauge paper-covered floral wire and an 8mm (0.3in) wide strip of the 160 grass-green crepe paper.

24 Stretch the strip of crepe paper out fully and attach and secure to the top of the wire with a light layer of glue.

25 Take one of the cut triangles and apply a little glue to the end of the piece. Place inside the strip so that it extends from the tip of the wire, then wrap around twice and add another triangle piece next to it. You can add further light amounts of glue as you go. Rotate the wire to the other side and place another triangle directly opposite the last one. Repeat the previous steps again until you have

around six pairs of leaves along the stem. Wrap a couple of times round the wire after the last leaf and then cut the paper and glue down. You don't need to continue to the end of the wire. Repeat to make additional leaves.

26 Once each leaf has been constructed, you can trim down the individual pieces with precision scissors to give each one a rounded point, and cut them so that they get very gradually larger as you get to the bottom of the leaf.

27 Attach the leaves to the main stem (see page 25), cutting the stem 1.5cm (0.60in) below the last leaf and adding them around a third of the way down the stem.

28 You can now style the flower and bend the stem as you wish, and have the outer petals sit evenly. You can also twist a few of the smallest inner petals around on themselves to give some variation to the centre of the flower.

25

27

Hydrangea

This is such a plush, romantic flower. It's inspiring to observe the different colour varieties of the flower in the natural world that you could experiment with. It's relatively easy in some ways to make a single floret from the bloom, although due to the nature of how many you need to make, it's good to make each flower part in batches to save you time.

You will need

180g Italian crepe paper in blues 556 and 615
160g German florist crepe paper in grass green
Doublette crepe paper in olive/ light olive
18-gauge floral wire
24 and 26-gauge paper-covered floral wire
Dr. Ph. Martin's Hydrus Watercolor in ultramarine red violet 36H
Standard scissors and precision scissors
Card, tracing paper and pencil for templates (see page 172)
Ruler
Wire cutters
Aleene's Original Tacky Glue
Watercolour paintbrush and water jar

We'll make the hydrangea from clusters of single florets placed together to make one bloom.

To make single florets

1 To make single florets, cut out 15 pieces of 180g blue 556 crepe paper measuring 10 x 5cm (4 x 2in) and fully stretch out as far as possible. Apply light washes of the watercolour to the sheets and refer to using watercolours on page 13. Make sure there are lots of subtle gradations of colour. Set aside to dry. You may need to colour more strips later if needed.

2 Take a 17cm (6.7in) length of 24-gauge paper-covered floral wire and a 5mm (0.2in) wide strip of the 180g darker blue 615 crepe paper. With a light layer of glue on the strip, wrap over and around the top of the wire and then continue to wrap to make a rounded oval piece on the end measuring around 1cm (0.40in) long and 2 to 3mm (0.08 to 0.12in) at the widest point.

3 Once your coloured paper is dry, cut out one of each of the four templates. Using the instructions on page 18 scrape your fingernail down the surface of each petal a few times to reduce the grain.

4 Place a small amount of glue at the base of each petal and wipe off any excess before placing at right angles around the centre.

5 Then stretch a 5mm (0.2in) wide strip of 160g grass-green crepe paper and with a light layer of glue, cover the top 5cm (2in) around the base of the flower. Then on a 45-degree angle, continue to cover the 5cm (2in) (see page 20 for wrapping stems).

6 To make a cluster of florets, we need to make 12 single florets. Once 12 florets have been made, take one of the florets and bend at a small angle at the 5cm (2in) mark down the stem. Then take a 7mm (0.3in) wide strip of 160g grass-green crepe paper and with a light layer of glue, place another floret against the first and secure with the strip, adding in another so they are all joined together at the 5cm (2in) mark. Keep the wrap of the strip as straight as possible. You can place in a few at a time before wrapping to reduce bulk. You can also place the flowers at very slightly different heights now and then to give a little variety.

1–3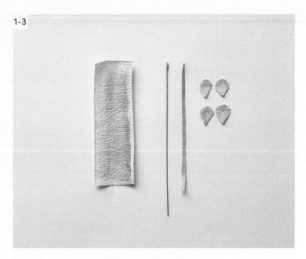

4

6

7 Once each floret is secure in the cluster, cut the floral wires down leaving just two at full length. The others can be cut directly underneath the strip that you used to secure them all. Then take another strip of the 160g grass-green crepe paper and wrap this over the bump that has been created to hide the ends of the wires. Cut and glue the strip down.

8 Repeat this to make one more cluster of florets in the same way and then make a third cluster where the stems all meet at the 4.5cm (1.8in) mark.

9 We need to make another three clusters, each joined at between the 3.5 to 4cm (1.4 to 1.6in) mark. Then to finish the shape of the flower, make five more smaller clusters with five florets each. Three of these florets need to be joined at the 2.5cm (1in) mark but with one or two florets in the cluster at 1cm (0.4in).

To assemble the flower

10 Take the three clusters that we made first with one of the stems meeting at 5cm (2in) placed in the centre. Place the other two clusters on either side, top of the florets all make a nice curve. Secure with a 1cm (0.4in) wide strip of the 160g grass-green crepe paper.

11 Then take the next three clusters and add these around on either side to create the round shape of the hydrangea. You can also add an 18-gauge piece of floral wire at this point to provide the main stem. Secure everything with the strip of crepe paper and a light layer of glue.

12 Next, the five smaller clusters can be added with the shorter florets sitting out on the bottom edge as far as possible. These clusters should sit nicely at the bottom and come in a little towards the centre of the bloom, hiding the wirework in the centre of the flower.

13 Cut down the stem wires again, leaving just one of the 24-gauge wires and the main 18-gauge wire. Cut the stem down to the desired length with wire cutters.

To make the stem and leaves

14 Wrap the stem tightly three times (see page 20), using a 1cm (0.40in) wide strip of the 160g grass-green crepe paper.

15 Make two leaves, one of each of the leaf templates, using the green doublette crepe paper cut on the bias (see page 23) and a piece of 26-gauge paper-covered floral wire. Flute the leaves with your fingers (page 18) on each side of the wire to give them a little movement. Cut down the leaf wires to 1cm (0.4in) below the base of the leaf.

16 Attach the leaves to the main stem (see page 25), one slightly lower than the other, using a 1cm (0.4in) wide strip of 160g grass-green crepe paper. Wrap down to the bottom of the stem if needed to ensure the stem looks a consistent width.

17 You can now style the flower by bringing down and opening up any petals at the base of the flower or within the flower itself to hide any wirework and give any petals more space if needed.

10

16

Honeysuckle

This brings back childhood memories as we had one climbing in our garden at home. I love the burst of the petals and the vibrant colour combination of the pink, red and yellow. A full vine of them would look amazing in paper too, so do experiment if you enjoy making them.

You will need

180g Italian crepe paper in deep pink 547

60g Italian crepe paper in yellow 292, pink 210 and green 264

Doublette crepe paper in olive/light olive

24 and 26-gauge paper-covered floral wire

20-gauge floral wire

White 1mm (0.04in) matt flower stamens

Green floral tape

Winsor & Newton Promarker in cocoa

Sennelier soft pastel in Chinese vermillion 790

Standard scissors and precision scissors

Card, tracing paper and pencil for templates (see page 171)

Ruler

Wire cutters

Aleene's Original Tacky Glue

Scalpel and ceramic dish

Pastel or cosmetic sponges and ceramic dish

To make a sprig of honeysuckle we need to make six florets, four large buds and five small buds for the main flower-head, and then two smaller clusters – one with five buds and one with six – and four leaves.

To make the florets

1 To make a floret, take four to five white flower stamens and colour the stamens on one end with the cocoa marker pen. Then hold them together and bring one stamen 1 to 1.5cm (0.4 to 0.6in) higher than the others. Cut straight across the stamens with scissors so that all the bottom stamens are removed.

2 Take a 7mm (0.3in) wide strip of 180g deep pink crepe paper and stretch between your fingers. Apply a light layer of glue to the top of the strip and fold over the top of a piece of 24-gauge paper-covered floral wire on a 45-degree angle.

3 Place the stamens on the strip so that about 4cm (1.6in) of them hang over the end of the wire, applying a little glue. Wrap the strip around tightly to cover the end of the stamens and then tear the strip and glue down.

4 Laminate a 5 x 6cm (2 x 2.4in) piece of 60g yellow crepe paper and a piece of 60g pink crepe paper together following the instructions on page 19. (You may need to laminate several pieces.) Cut out both petal pieces from the templates. Add a light layer of glue to the bottom 2cm (0.8in) of both pieces and glue them directly opposite each other around the stamens with the yellow on the inside, with the top of the pink wrap enclosing the stamens around about halfway down the petal. Using the closed blades of your precision scissors, curl the ends of the petals over gently. Cut the stem wire down to 7mm (0.3in). Repeat this to make six florets in total.

1-3

4

To make the buds

5 We use the same technique to make all the buds. For the main cluster, we need four large buds and five small buds. Take a piece of floral tape and cut with scissors down the length in the centre to make two thinner tape strips. Stretch a piece of the tape and fold over the top of a length of 24-gauge paper-covered wire. Wrap this around on a 45-degree angle down to the point when you would like the bud to end. Large buds range from 3.5 to 4.5cm (1.4 to 1.8in) in length. Smaller buds range from 2.5 to 3.5cm (1 to 1.4in).

6 Now bring the strip of tape carefully back up to the top of the bud on the 45-degree angle and then back down it, but this time wrapping to just before the bottom. Continue up and down the bud so that it gets larger at the top and gradually gets thinner at the base, ending in a point at the bottom. Once complete, large buds are around 5mm (0.2in) at the top and the smaller ones are about 3 to 4mm (0.1–0.2in). The shape of the bud should be consistent, and you can also use your fingers to help to mould a smooth shape.

7 Once you're happy with the shape of a bud, it can be covered in an 8mm (0.3in) wide strip of pink crepe paper. For the large buds we use a strip of the 60g pink crepe paper and for the smaller buds we use the 180g deep pink crepe paper.

8 File down some of the red pastel with a scalpel and then using a pastel sponge, smooth this over the top of the smaller buds only, graduating the colour down the upper-half of the bud.

9 You can now use the same process to make the buds for the two smaller clusters lower down. There are five buds on the left-hand cluster and six on the right. These are all around 3 to 3.5cm (1.2in to 1.4in) in length and 3 to 4 mm (0.1 to 0.2in) in thickness near the top. They are wrapped in the 180g deep pink crepe paper with the pastel added as well.

To make the leaves

10 Following the technique on page 23, make the four main leaves on the bias using the olive/light olive doublette crepe paper on a length of 26-gauge paper-covered floral wire. Cut each leaf wire stem down to around 1cm (0.4in). Gently flute the edges of each leaf following the instructions on page 18.

11 Tiny leaves are also hand-cut and placed at the base of each cluster. For the main cluster there are around seven, with a further two slightly larger ones placed just below on the main stem. For the two smaller clusters there are three to four tiny leaves on each. These are cut from the olive/light olive doublette crepe paper and are around 5 to 8mm (0.2 to 0.3in) in length.

5-8

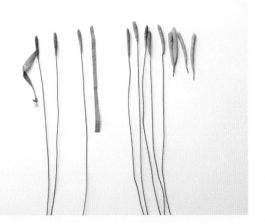

10-11

To bring the stem together

12 Take the five smaller buds and bend each one gently into a curved shape. Then with a stretched 5mm (0.2in) wide strip of 60g green crepe paper and a light layer of glue, wrap two of the buds so they meet at the base, taking care to use as little of the strip as possible to reduce bulk. Then add the remaining smaller buds as you wrap around. Tear and glue down the strip once all the small buds are secured together.

13 Next, add a few of the hand-cut tiny leaves underneath the cluster of small buds, gluing the base of these in place.

14 The larger buds can now be curved, and their stems cut down to 5mm (0.2in) then added in the same way, one by one, securing in place with a little glue and a lightly-glued strip of 60g green crepe paper. They can be added to the cluster 2mm (0.08 in) below the tiny leaves.

15 A few more tiny leaves can be added underneath these once they are secured and then the flowers can be added. These should be cut down to 5 to 7mm (0.2-0.3in) and given a curved shape as well, before being added. They should be spaced fairly evenly around the circle of other buds.

12

13

14

16 Once all the components are in place, we can wrap around underneath with the 60g green crepe paper to cover any excess wires. Again, we should be trying to limit the amount of wrapping we do to make sure it doesn't get bulky on the stem, but at the same time we want the stem to be a consistent thickness. Wrap down the stem to around 6.5cm (2.6in) – see page 20. Then tear off at this point, glue down and then re-wrap from the end of the bud wires to even out the stem and thicken where needed. A couple of larger 1cm (0.4in) long hand-cut leaves can be added at the point where the wire bulk ends to try to disguise it. You can cover the ends of the leaves with a piece of strip.

17 Add leaves one and two either side of the stem at the 6.5cm (2.6in) point and then wrap the stem further for another 4cm (1.6in).

18 Next, prepare the two small clusters in the same way as the previous small buds, although this time cutting down half on each cluster to a 5mm (0.2in) stem. Add a few tiny hand-cut leaves underneath each cluster and wrap the stems in the same way, keeping the thickness of the stems as even as possible. The left-hand cluster should have a stem of around 8cm (3in) long and the right-hand one around 4cm (1.6in). At this point cut the number of wires down in a staggered way to just one, again to reduce bulk (see page 25 on attching a leaf to a stem). Place the stem at an angle and wrap these into the main stem. When secured, add the remaining two leaves at the same point. You can now insert a piece of 20-gauge floral wire in the middle of the thinner wires to provide extra support for the long stem.

19 Cut the wire stems down at the point you would like it to end and wrap around 4 to 5 times to get a good thickness of around 3mm (0.1in).

20 You can now style the stem; bend it as you wish and adjust the placement of the clusters, buds and flowers.

Hollyhock

Hollyhocks are one of my absolute favourite flowers with their large papery petals. Feel free to experiment with the number of buds and blooms; there are no set rules when it comes to making this flower. This one is a labour of love, but it is worth it.

You will need

160g German florist crepe paper in grass green

180g Italian crepe paper in yellow 574, and shades of green 566 and 558 for all the flowers .

For the medium-pink hollyhock: 180g Italian crepe paper in pink 547 and Conté pastel pencil in violet 005 and lilac 026

For the cream hollyhock: 180g Italian crepe paper in cream 17A1 and Conté pastel pencil in light yellow 024 and St Michael green 044

For the burgundy hollyhock: 180g Italian crepe paper in burgundy 588 and Conté pastel pencil in purple 019 and sepia grey 042

1 and 1.5cm (0.40 and 0.60in) polystyrene balls

18 and 20-gauge floral wire

24-gauge paper-covered wire

3mm (0.10in) thick armature wire, 65cm (26in) length per flower

Green floral tape

Standard scissors and precision scissors

Card, tracing paper and pencil for templates (see page 175)

Ruler

Wire cutters

Hot glue and glue gun

Aleene's Original Tacky Glue

Scalpel

To make a single flower we will need to prepare the following components:

Seven x small buds

Three x large buds

One x unfolding bud

Three x small flowers

One x medium flower

Two x large flowers

Two x small leaves

Two x medium leaves

One x large leaf

To make the buds

1 To make a small bud, hot glue a 1cm (0.40in) polystyrene ball 5mm (0.20in) from the end of a piece of 20-gauge floral wire. Take a piece of floral tape, then stretch and wrap this around the ball and the end of the wire repeatedly, moulding and shaping with your fingers to form a teardrop shape. To add the calyx, cut six pieces from a piece of stretched 160g grass-green crepe paper, using the small bud template. Add glue to the bottom half of each piece. Glue the first three evenly around the bud, with the point level with the top of the bud. Then glue the last three over the gap that's between them. Cover a little of the wire below the bud, stretching out a 5mm (0.2in) wide strip of 160g grass-green crepe paper and wrapping it around with a little glue to cover 1.5cm (0.6in). Using wire cutters, trim each bud down to 2.5cm (1in).

2 To make a large bud, repeat this process, but this time use a 1.5cm (0.6in) polystyrene ball. Use the second bud template to add the greenery in the same way.

3 To make an unfolding bud, use floral tape to mould a 1.5cm (0.6in) length oval stamen shape (5mm/0.2in) at the widest point to the end of a length of 20-gauge floral wire. Take a 5mm (0.2in) wide strip of 180g yellow crepe paper and wrap this around to completely cover the stamen.

4 Next, take an 8 x 5cm (3 x 2in) piece of 180g crepe paper of your choice, stretch out fully and cut out three pieces from the unfolding petal template. Flute the top edges (see page 18) of all three petals and apply glue to the base. Place the first petal around the stamen, then add the second directly opposite, folding it around, then add the third to make unfolding petals.

5 Cut three calyx from stretched 160g grass-green crepe paper and glue these around the base of the bud. Wrap the stem with a 5mm (0.2in) wide strip of stretched 160g grass-green crepe paper and cover 1.5cm (0.6in) of the stem below.

1

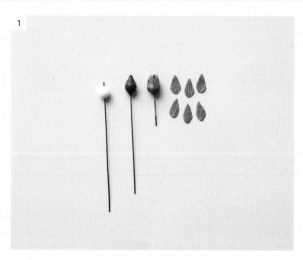

2

3–5

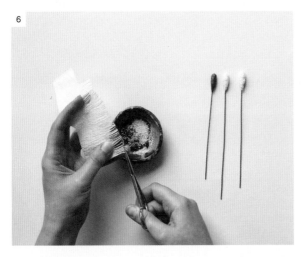

To make a flower

6 Take a 10cm long piece of 18-gauge floral wire, use floral tape to make an oval shape 2cm (0.8in) in length and 6mm (0.2in) (for the smaller/medium flowers) and 8mm (0.3in) (for the larger flowers) at the widest central point. Cover with a stretched-out 1cm (0.4in) wide strip of 180g yellow crepe paper to completely cover any tape. To add texture to the stamen, stretch out a piece of yellow crepe and finely fringe this with precision scissors. Then cut the fringe very finely from the side to make tiny flecks of pollen. Cover the stamen with glue and roll in the flecks of yellow to cover. Set aside to dry.

7 Next make a ledge to place the petals on by stretching out a 4 x 5cm (1.6 x 2in) piece of 180g lighter green 566 crepe paper, and laminating this twice by folding over and gluing all over, then gluing and folding over again (see page 19 on laminating). Cut out the ledge star shape from the four-layered paper.

8 Using the fine point of a scalpel, carefully make a small hole in the centre of the ledge. Then push the end of the stamen wire fully through the hole so that the ledge sits at the base of the stamen. Apply a little glue to the base of the stamen to hold the ledge in place.

9 To make the petals, cut these from the 180g crepe paper of your choice. You need to cut out five for each flower from the templates. Stretch out the paper fully. Apply pastel pencil firmly to the base of each petal, curving over the lower third of the base of the petal. Apply a little of the darker pastel pencil over the top if you're making the pink or burgundy flower, and the lighter pastel pencil if you're making the cream flower. Blend and smooth the colour out a little with your finger.

10 With the closed blades of your precision scissors, subtly curl the top half of each petal. Apply glue to the base of each petal and glue to the underside of the ledge, matching up the edges of the petal with the points of the ledge shape. Keep adding the petals to match these points as you go round.

11 Now we need to bring the petals forward and fix them in position. Apply a little glue to the bottom-right edge at the back of one petal and overlap the petal over the next petal by about a third. This will bring the petals forward. Continue around the flower, gluing the next petal to the next on the back edge, until all the petals are attached and brought forward into a bowl shape. You might need to adjust these a little here and there to get an even shape. You can now flute the edges of the petals deeply all around the flower to give the petals some variety.

12 Cut five calyx from stretched 160g grass-green crepe paper and glue these around the back of the flower-head. Stretch a 5mm (0.2in) strip of the 160g grass-green crepe paper and wrap this down the stem to cover 1.5cm (0.6in).

To make the leaves

13 Altogether we need two each of the small and medium leaves and one of the large. Follow the instructions on page 22 to make all these leaves on the bias, from the 160g grass-green crepe pape on 24-gauge floral wire. With these leaves, however, the grain of the paper needs to run down from the centre of the leaf rather than up. This is shown on the templates.

14 Cut a 5mm (0.2in) wide strip of 160g grass-green crepe paper and stretch, then with a light layer of glue, cover 1.5cm (0.6in) of the wire below each leaf. Trim down each leaf wire with wire cutters to 2.5cm (1in).

15 Curve the tops of the leaves lightly over the closed blades of your precision scissors.

To assemble the flower

16 Before assembling the flower, all the components should have their stems cut down to 2.5cm (1in) using wire cutters.

17 Then take a 65cm (26in) long piece of 3mm (0.1in) thick armature wire and straighten this out as much as possible. Cut a 1.5cm (0.6in) wide strip of 160g grass-green crepe paper and stretch this out, then with a light layer of glue, wrap and cover the whole length of the wire on a 45-degree angle (see page 20 on how to wrap a stem).

18 We will attach the buds first, in order of size. Take a 1cm (0.4in) strip of the 160g grass-green crepe paper and add a light layer of glue, then wrap this around the top of the wire and enclose the first small bud in your wrap, adding a little glue to the top of the bud stem. Continue to wrap around and down the stem, adding in further buds as you go. There are no set rules with placement, but we want the thickness of the stem to be consistent. I add small buds at 1cm (0.40in), 4cm (1.6in), 6.5cm (2.6in), 8cm (3.1in) and 9cm (3.5in). Then an unfolding bud and a large bud together at 11cm (4.3in). Next, the smallest flowers each at 17cm (6.7in) and 19.5cm (7.7in), a small leaf at 21cm (8.3in) and another small flower at 25cm (10in). Then at 28cm (11in) a small leaf and a large bud, then a medium flower at 31cm (12.5in). Next, add a medium leaf at 33cm (13in), a large flower at 37cm (14.5n), a medium leaf at 40cm (16in) and a large flower at 41.5cm (16.3in) and a final large leaf at 44.5cm (17.5in).

19 Wrap the remaining stem three or four times over to build up the thickness.

20 You can now style the whole flower, adjusting any individual flowers and leaves as you like.

Sweet pea 'King Tut'

These are a rare variety of sweet pea, rumoured to originate from seeds found in the tomb of Tutankhamun. They have a beautifully delicate and ephemeral feel, and the blue brings a lovely contrast in a display with other flowers. I would recommend trying this flower when you feel confident with wrapping stems as there is some intricate wire work involved.

You will need

180g Italian crepe paper in blue 615
160g German florist crepe paper in grass green
Doublette crepe paper in olive/ light olive
24-gauge green paper-covered floral wire
20-gauge floral wire
Spool floral wire
Conté pastel pencils in white 013 and vermillion 003
Standard scissors and precision scissors
Card, tracing paper and pencil for templates (see page 171)
Ruler
Wire cutters
Aleene's Original Tacky Glue

To make one stem I make three flowers.

To make the flowers

1 Take a piece of 24-gauge green paper-covered floral wire and a 5mm (0.2) wide strip of the 180g blue crepe paper, stretch the strip out fully and apply a little glue to the end of the strip. Attach this to the top of the floral wire on a 45-degree angle and apply a little more glue, then wrap down the wire for about 1.5cm (0.6in). Tear the paper and glue down to finish. Then take a pair of wire cutters and carefully use them to tightly bend over the covered end of the wire into a tiny hoop without cutting through the wire.

2 Cut three of the smaller petal templates out of stretched 180g blue crepe paper. Fold in half down the centre, scrape the outer edges of each petal inwards with your fingernail. Then apply white pastel pencil in a diamond shape at the base of the petal on both sides. Then fold the top edge over the closed blades of your precision scissors, so that the top edges fold into the centre. Apply a little glue to the base inside the fold and place the curved top of the floral wire at the base of the petal in the fold. Try to make sure the curved wire is as hidden as possible. Repeat this on two other separate pieces of wire for your other flowers.

3 Prepare to make three of your main petals by cutting 180g blue crepe paper squares on the bias, using the same technique as the making a leaf on the bias instructions on page 22, with the seam running down the centre of the petal. Cut out the petals and apply a half diamond of white pastel pencil to the lower third of the petal, then edge this with some of the vermillion pastel pencil. Fully glue down the seam on the back of each, take the closed blades of your precision scissors again and this time scrape the top of the petal over them so that the top edges turn outwards. Apply a little glue to the bottom of each petal and then place them directly behind the small petal. Repeat with the other two petals.

1–3

3-4

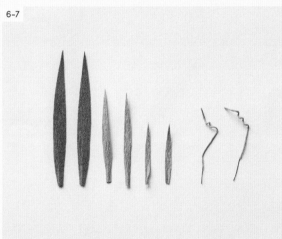

6-7

To make the calyx, leaves, stem

4 To make the calyx, cut a piece of 160g grass-green crepe paper 5 x 3cm (2 x 1.2in), stretch out fully and cut out three of the calyx from the template. Cut the base of the calyx down so that there is just 5mm (0.2in) remaining below the bottom of the calyx spikes. Apply a light amount of glue along the base and gather the piece as evenly as possible around the base of the petal that you've made, so that the spikes peek out around the bottom of the flower. Pinch together and roll between your fingers a little so that it all sits as neatly as possible. Repeat with the other two petals.

5 To prepare the petals to be attached to the stem, take a 5mm (0.2in) strip of 160g grass-green crepe paper and on a 45-degree angle cover 15cm (6in) of the wire below the calyx for one flower, and 4cm (1.6in) of the wire for both the others. Add a light layer of glue to the start of the strip and keep adding a small amount as you go, smoothing it over with your finger. Tear and glue down the strip once you cover the amount needed.

6 Next, you can prepare your leaves, and to do this you will need to laminate pieces of 160g grass-green crepe paper large enough to make two leaves each from leaf template 1 and 2. Stretch out the paper first and follow the instructions on page 19 for laminating paper. Then cut two leaves from leaf template 3, using the olive/light olive doublette crepe paper. Pinch each leaf in half at the base to bring it to a small point.

7 To make a tendril, take a 10cm (4in) piece of spool floral wire and cover the top 4 to 5cm (1.6 to 2in) with a 4mm (0.2in) wide strip of 160g grass-green crepe paper. This can take a little patience but if you get a good grip on the wire and the paper at the top, you should be able to wrap the same as any other wire. Tear and glue the paper down once you've covered the required amount. Then curl the covered part a little around a small piece of 18-gauge floral wire.

To assemble the flower

8 Take a length of 24-gauge green paper-covered floral wire and a 5mm (0.20 in) wide strip of 160g grass-green crepe paper. Stretch out the strip, then with a light layer of glue, attach the end on a 45-degree angle to the top of the wire. Fold over and then take the two smaller leaves made from laminated paper. Wrap these into the strip at the top of the wire, placing them opposite each other.

9 Continue wrapping the strip down the wire for 3cm (1.2in) and at this point you will add your first flower. Line up the flower so that it sits to the left of the main stem and the point where the crepe covering on the flower stem ends. Push the flower stem to the left on a 45-degree angle, apply a little glue at that point and wrap around this as you bring the strip down to cover the stem. Carry on wrapping for another 3.5cm (1.4in) and at this point you will wrap in the two tendrils opposite each other and the two medium leaves opposite each other at the same point. Once these have all been attached, you may need to increase the size of your wrapping strip to 7mm (0.3in) to account for the additional bulk. You may also need to start to wrap twice to cover the texture

of so many wires together. Try to keep all the wires as straight as possible as you wrap and try not to twist them.

10 Carry on wrapping further down the stem for another 3cm (1.2in), wrapping twice if you need to and then place the next flower to the right of the main stem. As before, line up the flower first and bend the stem 45 degrees to the right to attach it to the main stem. Once this has been secured, you can continue to wrap another 6cm (2.4in), and you will need to wrap twice at this point, where you now wrap in the remaining flower with the long, covered stem and the two large leaves opposite each other. This flower should sit in-between the other two. You can also wrap in a short piece of 20-gauge floral wire at this point to strengthen the stem.

11 Cut the stem wires at the point you would like the stem to end and then continue to wrap to the end of the stem. Repeat a few times to hide the texture of the wire and thicken the stem.

12 You can now style the flower. Gently curve the stems of the flowers and bring the flower-heads so they are facing forwards if you prefer.

English garden rose 'Darcey Bussell'

These roses have a really elegant shape and they're so satisfying to make in paper. In reality, the rose changes colour as it opens and starts to fade, so I've taken advantage of this in the colours I've selected to make it.

You will need

180g Italian crepe paper in the following colours:
For the magenta rose: 572
For the deep-red rose: 588
For the pink-purple rose: 590
For the leaves: dark green 591 and mid green 565
160g German florist crepe paper in grass green
18-gauge floral wire
24 and 26-gauge paper-covered floral wire
Dr. Ph. Martin's Hydrus Watercolors in ultramarine red violet 36H for the magenta and deep-red rose; deep red rose 4H for the pink-purple rose

Standard scissors and precision scissors
Card, tracing paper and pencil for templates (see page 174)
Ruler
Wire cutters
Aleene's Original Tacky Glue
Watercolour paintbrush, saucer and water jar

To make the inner petal section

1 Take a piece of 18-gauge floral wire and a 7mm (0.3in) piece of 180g crepe paper in your choice of flower colour. Stretch out your chosen crepe paper and add a light layer of glue at the top of the strip. Fold the strip over the end of the wire and then on a 45-degree angle cover the top 3cm (1.2in) of the stem. Repeat the covering again by reversing the wrap back to the top tightly and then cut and glue down and over the top of the wire.

2 Cut three pieces of 14 x 5cm (5.5 x 2in) in your chosen 180g crepe paper flower colour. Stretch out fully and cut in half. Then take the watercolour that corresponds to the paper colour you've chosen. Follow the instructions on page 13 on how to apply liquid watercolours and add a wash of colour to each piece. Leave to dry.

3 Cut out five of each of the first five petal templates. To make things easier, keep each petal size in separate piles when you have cut them out.

4 Now we need to make clusters of petals to form the centre of the flower. Take each of the five petals (one of each size) and apply a small amount of glue to the base of each one. Then place them on top of each other, in order of size, gluing the bases together. Then take the pile of petals and pinch them into a point at the base. Then fold a crease down the centre and scrape the crease with your thumbnail at the same time. Repeat to make five clusters in total.

5 Now we can attach the clusters to the main stem. Add a small amount of glue to the base of each cluster and then wipe off any excess. Take a cluster and place the base at the top of the floral wire. Push firmly against the wire to secure, then add the remaining clusters tightly at an even height around the central wire. You may need to pinch all the pieces together underneath several times to get them all to sit together securely. Let dry.

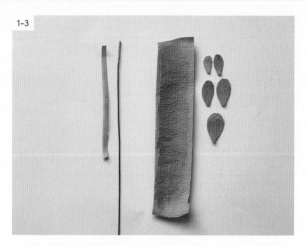

1–3

4

5

To make the outer petals

6 Once the central clusters are dry you can push them open and make sure they sit nicely. Cut out another three petals from template number 5 as before, but this time cup the petals deeply (see page 19) in the top half. You don't need to use the watercoloured paper at this point and can use the crepe paper straight from the original roll. Glue these three petals in some of the gaps between the clusters with a light layer of glue at the base. You also don't need to bring the petals to a point at the base; you can glue them straight on.

7 Next cut out eight petals from the petal 6 template and cup these deeply in the top half. Add these petals around the flower in any gaps and in-between petals to create a round shape around the clusters.

8 Once these have been added you can move on to cutting out 20 petals from petal template 7. Of the 20, 15 are heavily cupped in the top half and the remaining five will be added to the flower after the first 15; these will be only very lightly stretched out rather than cupped. Then place them to cover the in-between gaps produced by the upper layer of petals.

9 You can now cut out six petals from petal template 8. These will be lightly cupped and glued to the base of the flower in a convex shape, so the petals curve down rather than with the curve of the rest of the flower.

10 Once dry, to create a little asymmetry in the centre, take some of the smallest inner petals and twist them around on themselves a little so they don't all look quite the same.

To make the calyx, leaves and stem

11 Stretch a 5 x 5cm (2 x 2in) piece of 180g dark-green crepe paper almost fully between your fingers and cut five calyx pieces from the template. Then slit on each side with precision scissors along the dotted marks on the template. Glue the five calyxes underneath the flower at the point each petal overlaps with the one next to it.

12 Take a 1cm (0.4in) strip of 160g grass-green crepe paper and follow the instructions on page 20 for wrapping stems. Wrap the stem until you get a thickness of about 2mm (0.08in).

13 Next, we need to make the leaves. Follow the instructions for making leaves on the bias on page 22, and make the following using the templates:

14 For the larger sprig, you need one of the large leaf template, four of leaf template 2 and two of leaf template 3.

15 The medium sprig is one leaf from template 1 and two each of leaf templates 2 and 3.

16 The smallest sprig is one of leaf template 2 and four of leaf template 3.

17 Make the smallest sprig from 180g mid-green crepe paper and then make the two larger sprigs from 180g dark-green crepe paper.

18 Using precision scissors, cut fine 1mm (0.04in) lines or notches into the edge of each leaf and then pull these away out to the side to create a delicate shredded edge to the leaf.

19 Again following the instructions on page 22 for making leaves on the bias, place a piece of 24-gauge paper-covered floral wire inside each of the largest leaves in each sprig and the remaining leaves on 26-gauge paper-covered wire.

20 To put each sprig together, see page 24 on how to do this. Use a 5mm (0.2in) thick strip of 160g to wrap the leaves together, adding them at the 1.0cm to 1.5cm (0.4 to 0.6in) point and the again at the 2.5cm (1in) point. Then wrap down the stem for a further 2.5cm (1 in). Make sure the stems are trimmed down and bent (see page 25).

11

13–16

21 Once all the leaves are added, bend the stem at 45 degrees so it can be placed on the main flower stem. Cut the wires down in short, staggered lengths to reduce bulk on the stem. Repeat to make the other two leaf sprigs.

22 To attach the leaf sprigs to the main stem, use a 1cm (0.4in) strip of stretched 160g grass-green crepe. Place the first (medium) sprig on the side of the flower stem around 9cm (3.5in) down. See page 23 for guidance. Continue down the stem for 4cm (1.6in) and then add the large leaf sprig on the left. Continue wrapping for the next 2.5cm (1in) and then add the smallest leaf sprig on the right. Wrap to the end of the stem. Repeat again to conceal wires if necessary and wrap below the wires to give a consistent thickness to the stem if needed.

23 You now have your completed rose and you can style the stem and leaves to finish. Bend the flower-head forward slightly, shape the stems into a gentle curve. You can fold the leaves in a little to give some movement.

Hybrid Tea rose

One of my most requested workshops is for a classic rose, so it was an easy decision to include how to make these roses in dusky, vintage colours. You could also try mixing up the colours of the leaves with different shades of green to give some variety.

You will need

180g Italian crepe paper in the
    following colours:
For the medium-pink rose:
    17A4 and 20E1
For the dark, dusky-pink rose:
    547 and 620
For the light-peach rose: 17A4
    and 569
For the red rose: 586 and 589
For the leaves: dark green 17A8
160g German florist crepe paper
    in grass green
18-gauge floral wire
2cm (0.8in) polystyrene balls
24 and 26-gauge paper-covered
    floral wire
Standard scissors and precision
    scissors
Card, tracing paper and pencil
    for templates (see page 172)
Ruler
Wire cutters
Hot glue and glue gun
Aleene's Original Tacky Glue

To make the centre

1 To make a base for the petals, hot glue a 2cm (0.8in) polystyrene ball to the end of a length of 18-gauge paper-covered floral wire.

2 To cover the polystyrene, cut a rectangle of one of the 180g crepe paper flower colours that you are using, measuring 2 x 5cm (0.8 x 2in). Stretch this out fully and apply a light layer of glue over the whole surface. Place the centre of the paper over the centre of the polystyrene ball and gather it around the ball, moulding into a neat covering over and underneath.

1–2

To make the petals

3 We need to laminate the two colours together for each petal individually and then work with them straightaway to make the rose. This is because they are malleable when still a little damp from the glue.

4 To make a petal, take a 5cm (2in) wide strip of each pair of your chosen 180g crepe paper flower colour and stretch this fully between your fingers. Place both strips on top of one another and your petals template on top of them. Cut a square around the template, leaving a little distance round the edges. See the instructions on page 19 for laminating paper and glue the two pieces together. Cut out the petal from the template. After each petal has been attached to the rose, you can repeat this to make the next petal. In total, we need three petals from template 1, five petals from template 2, three petals from template 3 and six petals from template 4.

5

6

7

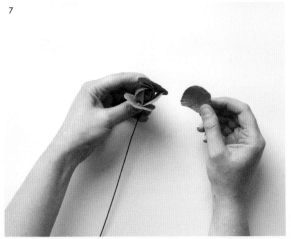

To place each petal on the flower

5 TEMPLATE 1: cup each petal in the centre and apply a light layer of glue to the bottom half. Smooth this over with your finger and then apply the petal around the centre ball, ensuring that the base of the `groove' in the petal sits in the centre of the ball, raised above it so it gives the centre a point. Smooth all the edges down and around the base. Repeat with the next two petals at right angles, so that you form a tiny circle in the centre.

6 TEMPLATE 2: cup each petal in the lower half and gently scrape the very top of the edges over the closed blades of your precision scissors. You can cut a tiny, uneven line along the top edge. Place the first one so that the top edge sits 3mm (0.1in) from the edge and slightly above the tiny centre circle. Smooth the petal down around the base. Repeat with the remaining petals, adding these 1.5cm (0.6in) clockwise from the position of the previous petal. Try to keep the shape of the point in the centre and let the last petal come away from the others slightly.

7 TEMPLATE 3: Repeat the cupping and treatment of the edges as per template 2. Apply a light layer of glue to the bottom third of each petal. Add the first two petals opposite each other, with one sitting in the gap in-between the swirl of previous petals and then the other glued directly opposite. These should sit about level with the previous petals but come away from the centre more. Add the third petal to the left of the previous one, at eleven o'clock if you imagine the flower as a clock, with the previous two sitting at seven and one o'clock.

8 TEMPLATE 4: repeat the cupping and treatment of the edges again as before and apply glue to the lower quarter of each petal, then add the first two petals to the flower in the gaps at three and nine o'clock. For the last four petals you can use a short piece of 18-gauge floral wire to tightly roll the top edges a little to create a tighter shape. Then these four can be placed at five, seven, eleven and one o'clock.

To make the calyx, leaves and stem

9 Stretch a 5 x 5cm (2 x 2in) piece of 180g dark-green crepe paper almost fully between your fingers and cut five calyx pieces from the template. Use the calyx template from the Garden Rose tutorial. Then slit on each side with precision scissors along the dotted marks on the template. Glue the five calyxes underneath the flower at the point each petal overlaps with the one next to it.

10 Cut the main flower stem with wire cutters to the length you require.

11 Take a 1cm (0.40in) strip of 160g grass-green crepe paper, stretch between your fingers, apply glue to the end and wrap the stem a few times, following the instructions on page 20.

12 To make the leaves, see making leaves on the bias on page 22. You can use the leaf templates from the Garden Rose tutorials. Use the 180g dark green crepe and cut out one of leaf number 1 template and three of each of the number 2 and 3 templates. Place the large leaf and a number 2 leaf on 24-gauge paper-covered wires and the remainder on 26-gauge.

13 Using precision scissors, cut fine 1mm (0.04in) lines or notches into the edge of each leaf and then pull these away out to the side to create a delicate shredded edge to the leaf.

14 For the larger sprig, you need one of leaf template 1, and two each of leaf template 2 and 3. With the smaller sprig it is one of template 2 and 3.

15 Follow the instructions for making a multiple-leaf sprig on page 24. To make each sprig use a 5mm (0.2in) thick strip of 160g grass-green crepe paper to wrap them together. For the main sprig, place the first two leaves after about 1cm (0.40in) and then the final 2 leaves after another 2.5cm of wrapping the stem. Then you can wrap for a further 3.5cm (1.4in) where you can tear the strip and glue down.

16 You can make the smaller leaf sprig in the same way, this time ending the wrapping of the sprig 2cm (0.8in) from the base of the last leaf to make it shorter.

17 To attach the leaf stem to the main stem, apply a little glue to the edge of the leaf stem and place on the side of the flower stem around 9cm (3.5in) down. Take a strip of stretched 160g grass-green crepe about 1cm (0.4in) wide, and with a light layer of glue, wrap this around the leaf stem to secure in place. Continue down the stem on a 45-degree angle for 1cm (0.40in) and then add the smaller leaf sprig you prepared and put together in the same way. Continue wrapping to the end of the stem. Repeat again to conceal wires if necessary and wrap below the wires to give a consistent thickness to the stem if needed.

18 You now have your completed rose and you can style the stem and leaves to finish. Bend the flower-head forward, shape the stems from the point they meet and adjust any petals to open up the rose and ensure the petals sit nicely.

15

17

Projects

Now that we've explored making single stem flowers, we can move on to explore ways we can display them, either in the home or for a special event. In this section, we look at how to bring the flowers together in a bouquet and arrangement, and how to make a pretty wall hanging, table setting and mini wreaths.

Some new flowers have been introduced, alongside the flowers that we've learnt previously, and some new variations on those flowers too. There are also some new types of foliage to learn about and incorporate in the designs. I hope you find this section useful, and the projects are a good catalyst for your own ideas and creativity in elevating your flowers.

Wild rose table setting

This beautiful wild rose has a natural and very gradual blend of colour on the petals and makes good use of the lovely colour of the peach crepe paper. These would make a beautiful addition to a dinner table setting and you could place some on longer stems and in small vases too.

You will need

180g Italian crepe paper in mustard 579, yellow 17E5, medium green 622 and dark green 17A8

Doublette crepe paper in white/apricot

160g German florist crepe paper in grass green

20-gauge floral wire

24 and 26-gauge paper-covered floral wire

Winsor & Newton Promarker in burnt sienna

Sennelier soft pastels in yellow 098 and peach 684

Standard scissors and precision scissors

Card, tracing paper and pencil for templates (see page 171)

Ruler

Wire cutters

Aleene's Original Tacky Glue

Scalpel and 2 ceramic dishes

Pastel or cosmetic sponges

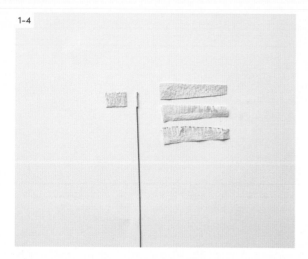

1–4

10

To make the centre

1 Cut a 5 x 3cm (2 x 1.2in) piece of 180g mustard crepe paper, stretch fully between your fingers and cut the centre template out. With precision scissors, finely fringe the top edge of the cut piece 1mm (0.04in) deep (see fringing on page 18).

2 Apply a thin layer of glue to the uncut part of the fringed strip and wrap tightly around the top of a length of 20-gauge floral wire, with the top of the wire lying flush at the bottom of the fine fringe, securing with glue at the end.

3 Cut a separate 7 x 3cm (2.8 x 1.2in) piece of the 180g yellow crepe paper, stretch fully out again and cut the stamen fringe template out. Very finely fringe the paper from the top down to the dotted line on the template. The finer you can cut this fringe, the better the flower will look.

4 Next, twist the fringe between your fingers gently to create texture. Apply a very light amount of burnt sienna marker pen to the very tip of the fringe, taking care as the colour will bleed.

5 Then apply a thin layer of glue to the left-bottom corner at the shortest end and roll around the top of the centre stem, with the bottom of the fringe on both pieces of crepe paper lining up. Secure with glue at the end.

6 Tease out the fringe with the precision scissors to expose the centre slightly. Add more marker pen or cut out some of the colour if there is too much. Trim so it looks uniform.

To make the petals

7 Take an 11 x 11cm (4.3 x 4.3in) piece of white/apricot doublette crepe paper and cut out five petals per flower from the template.

8 We'll now add pastel to the petals and you can see page 12 on how to do this. Add a gentle gradation of yellow pastel on to the bottom third of each petal. Then use the peach pastel in the same way with a separate sponge to apply a little gradation to the top third of the petals.

9 Cup the petals individually over the curve of the back of your thumbs in the bottom third of the petal. Then towards the top of the petal, shape the top edge of each petal gently over the closed blades of your precision scissors. See page 19 for cupping and curling.

10 Apply a little glue to the base of the petals and place around the centre, directly below the fringe of the centre. Overlap them very slightly so that all petals are evenly glued around the centre. Pinch around underneath the flower to secure them.

To make the calyx, leaves and stem

11 Stretch a 5 x 3cm (2 x 1.2in) piece of 180g medium-green crepe paper fully between your fingers and cut five calyx pieces from the template. Then make a slit on each side with precision scissors along the dotted marks on the template. Glue the five calyxes underneath the flower at the point each petal overlaps with the one next to it.

11

12 Cut the main flower stem with wire cutters to the length of around 17cm (6.7in) to make a table setting flower.

13 Take a 1cm (0.4in) wide strip of 180g medium-green crepe paper, stretch between your fingers, apply glue to the end and wrap around directly underneath the flower-head to cover any excess paper underneath. Then bring the strip down the stem at a 45-degree angle, adding a light layer of glue as you go until you reach 5.5cm (2.2in) down the stem. Rip and glue down the paper at this point and then wrap again to the 5.5cm (2.2in) point so that the stem that is covered is a consistent thickness.

14 At this point, you can push the flower-head of the flower forward with a tight curve behind it and open out the petals evenly so you can start to see where to place your leaves.

14–15

15 To make the leaves, see making leaves on the bias page 22, and make three leaf sprigs, one from each of the heavyweight crepe papers (180g medium and dark green and 160g grass-green).

16 Sprig 1 (smallest sprig) consists of one x leaf template 2 and two x leaf template. Sprigs 2 and 3 consist of one x leaf template 1, two x leaf template 2 and two x leaf template 3. Two of the large leaf sprigs should have a 2.5cm (1in) covered stem that joins to the flower and the smallest should have a 2cm (0.8in) stem. Cut tiny notches with the precision scissors into the edge of the leaves and then pull out from the leaf to give a serrated edge. To put each sprig together, see the instructions for making a rose leaf on page 146.

16

17 Attach the smallest leaf stem at the 5.5cm (2in) point on the left of the main stem with a 1cm (0.4in) wide strip. Then wrap a further 3.5cm (1.4in) down the main stem. You might need to repeat this again if the wires show through the paper too much. Attach a second sprig on the right at this point. Then wrap again for another 3.5cm (1.4in) and place the final sprig in at this point. You can now wrap to the end of the stem and repeat a few times until you have a consistent thickness. Now you can style the stem; bending it and the leaf sprigs in to gentle curves and adjusting the placement of the petals if needed.

Mini cherry blossom wreaths

These delicate cherry blossom wreaths can be made with as many flowers as you like, and you can vary the size of the wreath too. To save time in making the flowers you can work in batches and make several blossoms at the same time. Once you've learnt how to make them you could even make them into a branch.

You will need

180g Italian crepe paper in red 586, deep pink 547 and brown 568. Then you can choose your light shade of pink between 569, 548 and 549

160g florist crepe paper in grass green

24 and 26-gauge paper-covered floral wire

20-gauge floral wire

Yellow-tipped 1mm (0.04in) matt flower stamens, or use white stamens and colour the tips with Winsor & Newton Promarker in sunflower

8mm (0.31in) plastic beads

Sennelier soft pastel in Chinese vermillion 790

Standard scissors and precision scissors

Card, tracing paper and pencil for templates (see page 172)

Ruler

Wire cutters

Hot glue gun and hot glue

Aleene's Original Tacky Glue

Short, thin paintbrush

1cm (0.4in) wide silk ribbon

To make one wreath you will need to make:

12 cherry blossoms

Four buds

Two small leaves

One medium leaf

Two large leaves

To make a cherry blossom

1 Cut a 3 x 2cm (1.2 x 0.8in) piece of 180g red crepe paper and stretch fully between your fingers. Take the centre template and cut out one piece. Finely fringe one of the long edges with precision scissors 1mm (0.04in) deep (see fringing on page 18). Repeat this again with the 180g deep-pink crepe paper to make a second fringed piece.

2 Place a little glue on the bottom-left side of the red piece. Take a 12cm (4.7in) long piece of 24-gauge paper-covered floral wire and place the top point at the base of the fringe. Wrap around the top of the wire tightly and glue at the end to secure.

3 Take five stamens and colour the tips with marker if you don't have yellow stamens. Fold in half. Take the deep-pink strip and add a light layer of glue to the bottom left. Place the fringe 1mm (0.04in) above the top of the red fringe and take three of the folded stamens. Place these inside the strip so that the stamens sit about 1.5cm (0.6in) above the centre. Wrap around slightly with the stamens enclosed and then add the remainder as evenly as possible opposite. Tear and glue down the strip after it has been wrapped once around the centre. Cut the bottom of the stamens off with scissors.

4 Next, stretch a 6 x 3.5cm (2.4 x 1.4in) piece of the 180g light-pink crepe paper of your choice and cut five petals per flower using the petal template. You can accordion-fold the paper to make this quicker.

5 Place a thin layer of glue at the base of each petal and twist between your fingers to bring it to a tight point. Apply another layer of glue to the twisted base and glue around the centre evenly just below the base of the fringing. To cover the base of the petals, cut a 7mm (0.3in) strip of 160g grass-green crepe paper, stretch fully, and with a light layer of glue, wrap this around the base of the petals and on a 45-degree angle down the stem covering 1cm (0.4in) of the wire.

6 Once completely dry, take a small paintbrush and rub directly on to the red pastel, then apply the lightest amount around the centre. You only need a small amount to give a little depth to the colour.

7 Repeat the above to make 12 cherry blossoms in total.

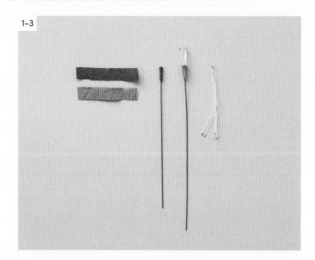

1–3

5

5

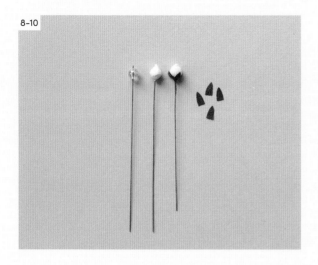

8–10

To make a bud

8 Hot glue an 8mm (0.3in) plastic bead to a 12cm (4.7in) piece of 26-gauge paper-covered floral wire, leaving 2mm (0.08in) of wire poking through the top of the bead.

9 Take a 1cm (0.4in) wide strip of your chosen 180g light-pink crepe paper and with a light layer of glue, wrap this around the bead and the wire to create a bud, smoothing and pinching the paper with your fingers to create a neat shape. For the calyx, stretch out a 3 x 2cm (1.2 x 0.8in) piece of 180g brown crepe paper and cut out four from the calyx template. Apply a little glue to the base of each one and glue these around the base of the bud.

10 Then take a 5mm (0.2in) strip of the 180g brown crepe paper stretched out and cover the top 1cm (0.4in) of the stem wire, then tear the paper and glue down. Cut the bud stem down to 2cm (0.8in). Repeat to make four buds in total.

To make a leaf

11 We need two small leaves, one medium and two of the large leaves. To make the leaves, we use a length of 26-gauge paper-covered floral wire this time and the 160g grass-green crepe paper. Cut the leaves on the bias as per the instructions on page 22. Leave the wire stem bare but cut down to 2cm (0.8in).

11

To bring the blossoms together

12 Take a 35cm (14in) 20-gauge piece of floral wire and a stretched-out 1cm (0.40in) width piece of brown crepe paper. Apply a light layer of glue to the top of the strip and wrap around the top of the floral wire. Bring down the strip on a 45-degree angle as per the instructions on how to wrap stems on page 20.

13 After the first 3cm (1.2in) add in a bud, placing it against the branch by bending the stem on the bud to an angle and applying a little glue to position it in place. Wrap underneath the bud with the lightly-glued strip. Then continue down the branch and after 2cm (0.80in), add the second bud on the opposite side of the wire.

14 Add the first blossom 2cm (0.8in) after this, then a small leaf after 1.5cm (0.6in), another blossom after 1cm (0.4in), then another blossom 1.5cm (0.6in) after

this. Continue down the branch, adding blossoms and leaves 1 to 2cm (0.40 to 0.80in) apart, trying to keep things a little asymmetrical so that they look natural. Finish the branch stem with the final buds. Wrap to the end of the branch and tear and glue down the end.

15 Bend the branch into a curved horseshoe shape. Then take a length of 26-gauge paper-covered floral wire and wrap this with a 5mm (0.20in) stretched strip of 180g brown crepe paper. Use this to connect the two ends of the blossoms, wrapping it tightly around each side to secure. Cut it down if the piece is too long.

16 You can now add a piece of 1cm (0.4in)-wide silk ribbon to the base of the wreath. Adjust the flowers and leaves as you wish and open them up fully if you like, making sure the blossoms point in different directions to give variety and aren't grouped together too symmetrically.

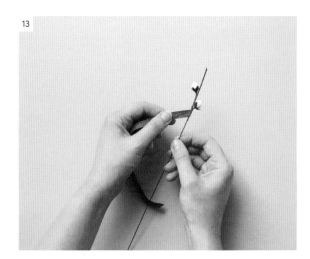

Peony & tulip arrangement

This asymmetric arrangement contains a sweet mix of peonies, tulips and sweet peas. It's perfect for placing against a wall in your home and brightening a space. It's best not to use floral foam as it isn't good for the environment, so this has been made with a ceramic bowl and a flower frog. I've taken a little creative licence with the sweet peas and tulips and made them in different colours to previous tutorials. This ensures the colours blend nicely.

You will need to make and gather in advance

4 x Bowl of Beauty peonies (see page 80): one with two small peony leaves sitting on the right of the stem and the other three peonies with no leaves attached.

3 x sweet pea stems (see page 130) made with 180g Italian crepe paper in pink 620

5 x tulips (see page 58) with one leaf each made with 180g Italian crepe in pink 17A3 and coloured and blended around the stamens with Conté pastel pencil in yellow 004

7 x peony leaf sprigs (of three leaves) from the Bowl of Beauty peony tutorial, coloured at the edges and then blended with Dr. Ph. Martin's Hydrus Watercolor in deep red rose 4H

160g German florist crepe paper in grass green

15cm (6in) wide ceramic bowl

6cm (2.4in) flower frog/pin

Aleene's Original tacky glue

Wire cutters

To put the arrangement together

1 Cut down the stems of the peony leaf sprigs so that they will overhang the edges of your bowl. Place two sprigs at the front of the arrangement on either side of the centre and the remainder around the rest of the bowl. You may need to thicken the base of the stems with a 1cm (0.4in) strip of the 160g grass-green crepe paper and a light layer of glue until they are thick enough to be held securely by the flower frog.

2 Next, add the four peonies. Cut the stem to around 32cm (13in) for the tall Peony with the leaves so it has a good amount of height. The focal peony at the front can be cut so that it sits snugly above the rim of the bowl but doesn't come too far forward. Then the third peony that faces towards the back right can be cut so that it sits slightly above the peony at the front. A fourth Peony gets placed at the back left and faces that way too, sitting snugly over the rim of the bowl. Place the peonies into the arrangement with the tall flower at a slight forward angle, the front peony facing forwards.

1

2

3 The tulips can be added next, and the petals splayed open on four of the stems to expose the stamen. One tulip should sit to the top left of the front peony and another curving down on a longer stem towards the base. The next short-stem tulip then gets placed over the rim of the bowl facing towards the back-left of the arrangement. Another then curves gently in front and across the base of the tall peony. A short-stemmed tulip with petals closed then gets placed amongst the foliage, hidden behind the front-facing peony.

4 We can now add the sweet peas, with one stem facing away towards the back next to the peony; one stem curving gently to the left; and another to the right of the tall peony.

Poppy wall hanging

This hanging really shows off the poppy flower and its distinctive curved stem and bud. You could make your hanging as large or small as you need it to be, and you can add as many flower layers as the top of the hanging can support.

You will need to make and gather in advance

20 or more Icelandic poppies (see page 62) in various colours and on stems of various lengths
Poppy buds made with 1 and 1.5cm (0.4 and 0.6in) polystyrene balls on stems of various lengths
160g German florist crepe paper in grass green
Wire cutters
Roll of string

To put together the wall hanging

1 Tie a piece of string tightly between two wall fastenings.

2 Gather your selection of poppies and buds. With a 1cm (0.4in) strip of 160g grass-green crepe paper, attach some of the buds to the flower stems at various points so all the flower stems don't look the same. Bend the buds so that they have a distinct curve. Often the poppy bud loops back on itself parallel with the stem. You can also leave some bud stems on their own with no flowers.

3 With your wire cutters, curve over the end of each stem to create a small hook.

4 Hang the stems on the string, ensuring the flower-heads sit at different points and the flowers don't all hang at the same height. You can cut down the stems if you find too many flowers sit at the same point. Try to make sure the flowers face forwards as much as possible.

5 Once the first stems have been placed on the hanging, you can add a second and third level, hanging these flowers from hooks on the flower-heads or bud stems above.

6 Continue hanging more layers of flowers to fill the space that you have.

Summer mixed bouquet

For a very special occasion or even as a gift, you can bring together a mix of paper flowers into a beautiful summer bouquet.

You will need to make and gather the following flowers in advance as well as make some additional foliage. Each piece should be made on as long a stem as possible.

8 x English garden roses (see page 136)
3 x Bowl of Beauty peony flowers (see page 80)
4 x Cupcake cosmos flowers (see page 108)
4 x wild rose flowers (see page 150)

Further materials needed:

180g Italian crepe paper in dark green 17A8
160g German florist crepe paper in grass green
26-gauge floral wire
20-gauge floral wire

Chicken wire
2cm (0.8in)-wide silk ribbon
Card, tracing paper and pencil for templates (see page 175)

To put together the bouquet:

1 Mould a piece of chicken wire into a cylindrical piece measuring 9 x 5 cm (3.5 x 2 in).

2 Now we need to make a foliage base for the bouquet. Make sprigs of ruscus leaves using the leaf templates (see page 175), wiring each leaf on to a piece of 26-gauge wire and then wrapping them all together in to one stem. Place the leaves opposite each other and around the stem randomly. Make 5 sprigs in a mix of both 180g and 160g green crepe papers. Add a variety of leaves on each stem with one with 12 leaves and the reminder a mix between 4 and 6.

3 To make the long whispy pieces of foliage, cut a 3 x 25cm (1.2 x 1in) piece of 180 dark-green crepe paper and stretch out fully. Fold in half with the grain and cut a folded piece 1 cm (0.4in) thick. Laminate both sides together with a piece of 20-gauge floral wire placed inside in the centre of the laminated strip. Cut a freehand long thinly tapered leaf shape. Wrap the stem a few times with the 160g grass-green crepe paper. Curve the pieces gently into a nice shape with your fingers.

4 Place the ruscus leaves into the floral wire, with the longest pieces on the left-hand side, then further sprigs placed at the top, on the right-hand side and then at the back towards the base of the wire towards the left and right.

5 Next, add the garden rose flowers, with a deep red flower placed at the front left, the two purple pinks to the right of this one and another of these just behind. Place the flowers so that they sit snugly together on top of the wire. Then add a magenta rose over the top of the two purple roses. Add a further 2 deep red roses at the back, on both the left and right of the chicken wire, with a purple/pink rose in-between. Make sure to try to point the flowers so that they face in different directions.

6 Next add the three Bowl of Beauty peony flowers, with two at the front of the bouquet, one towards the top-left facing to the left and another on the bottom-right facing to the right. A third flower is placed at the back in the centre.

7 Now we can add the Cosmos flowers. These are placed to the bottom left of the first peony and another at the bottom right. Then a third is placed at the top right, coming away a little from the other flowers and facing forwards. A last Cosmos is placed at the back behind the last and underneath a dark rose.

8 Next, we can place in the wild roses. The first can be placed at the base of the front of the bouquet next to the red rose. Then the next three are placed away from the main flowers a little, with one leaning above and to the right, another across the right above the peony and a third off-centre to the left. You can face these in different directions to give variety.

9 You can now add in the whispy foliage, placing them around the top of the bouquet, making sure the curves of the leaves fall nicely amongst the flowers.

10 Finally, you can tie a silk ribbon to the base of the bouquet, so that it hangs nicely from the flowers.

Templates

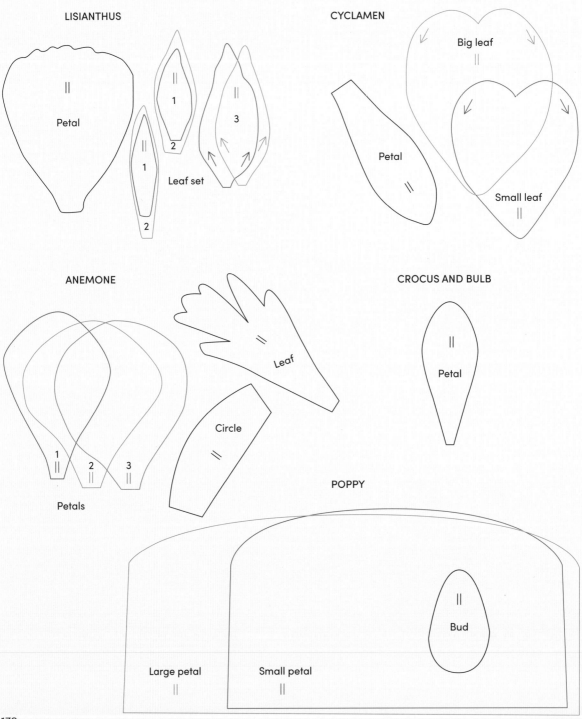

LISIANTHUS

Petal

‖

1
2
Leaf set

1
2

‖

‖

1

2

‖

3

CYCLAMEN

Big leaf
‖

Petal
‖

Small leaf
‖

ANEMONE

Leaf
‖

Circle
‖

1
‖

2
‖

3
‖

Petals

CROCUS AND BULB

Petal
‖

POPPY

Bud
‖

Large petal
‖

Small petal
‖

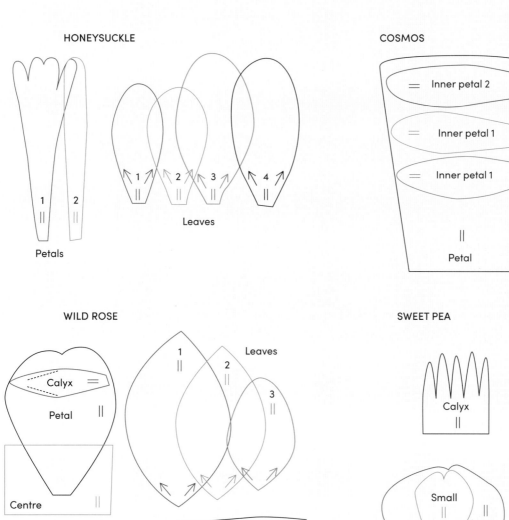

HONEYSUCKLE

Petals

1 2

Leaves

1 2 3 4

COSMOS

Inner petal 2

Inner petal 1

Inner petal 1

Petal

WILD ROSE

Calyx

Petal

Centre

Leaves

1 2 3

Stamen fringe

SWEET PEA

Calyx

Small Large

Petals

Leaves

1 2 3

LILY REGALE

Petals

1 2

Leaves

1 2

Bud

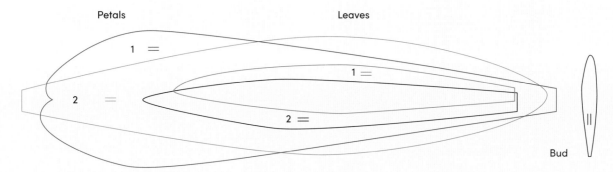

HYDRANGEA

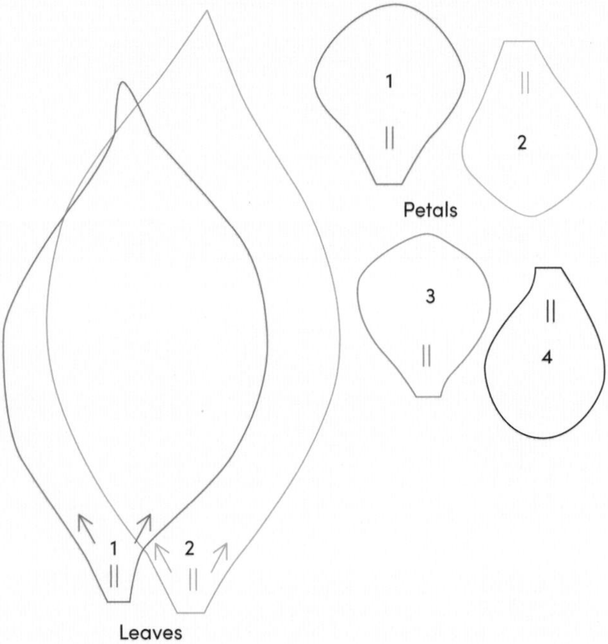

1

2

Petals

3

4

1

2

Leaves

CHERRY BLOSSOM

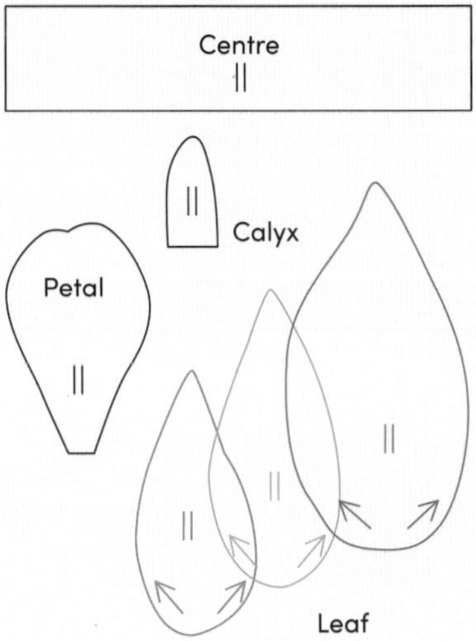

Centre

Calyx

Petal

Leaf

TULIP

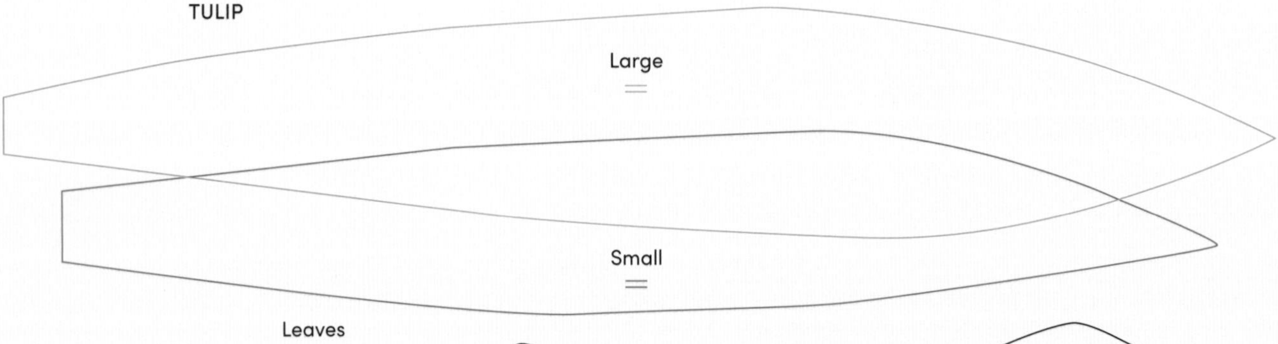

Large

Small

Leaves

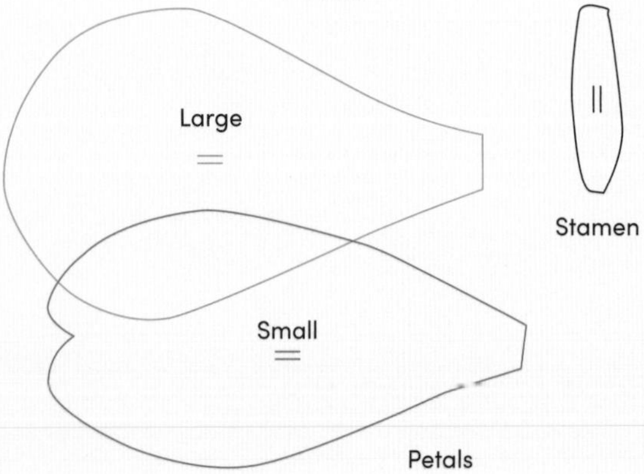

Large

Stamen

Small

Petals

TEA ROSE

4

1

2

3

Petals

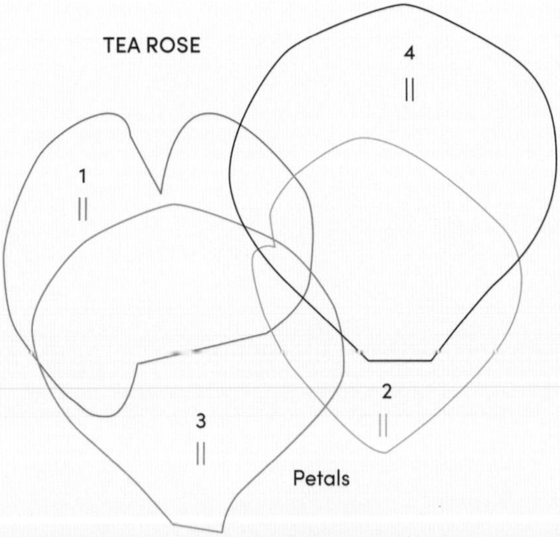

CORAL CHARM PEONY

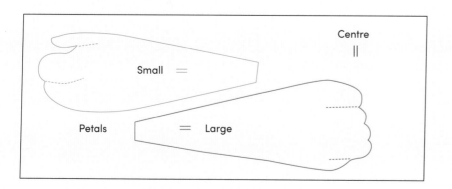

Centre ||

Small =

Petals

= Large

BOWL OF BEAUTY PEONY

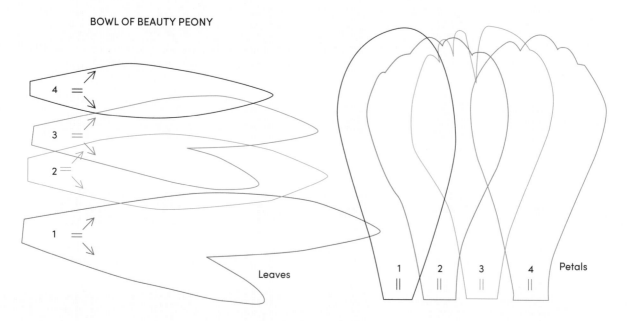

4 =

3 =

2 =

1 =

Leaves

1 ||

2 ||

3 ||

4 ||

Petals

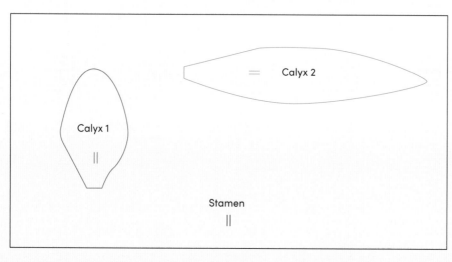

= Calyx 2

Calyx 1

||

Stamen

||

GARDEN ROSE

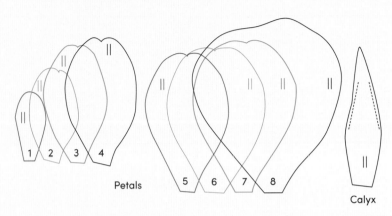

Petals

Calyx

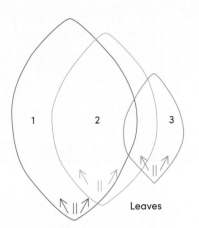

Leaves

SEMI CACTUS DAHLIA

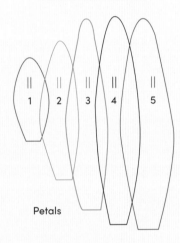

Petals

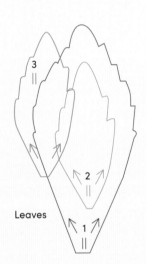

Leaves

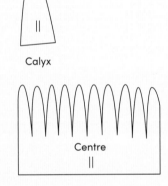

Calyx

Centre

FUCHSIA BRANCH

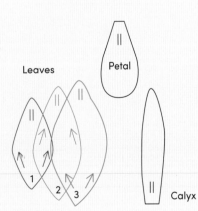

Leaves

Petal

Calyx

NARCISSUS

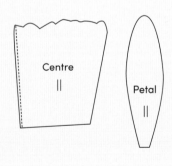

Centre

Petal

CAFE AU LAIT DAHLIA

SUMMER BOUQUET

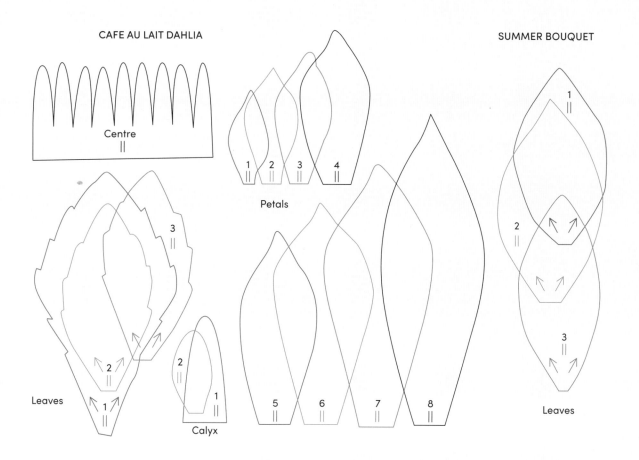

Centre
||

Petals

1   2   3   4
|| || || ||

1
||

2
||

3
||

Leaves

3
||

2
||

1
||

Calyx
2   1
|| ||

5   6   7   8
|| || || ||

Leaves

HOLLYHOCK

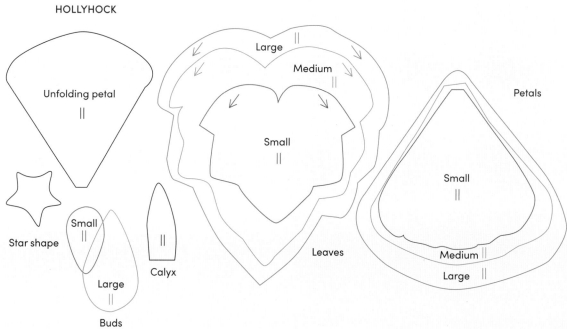

Unfolding petal
||

Large
||

Medium
||

Small
||

Petals

Star shape

Small
||

Large
||

Buds

Calyx
||

Leaves

Small
||

Medium
||

Large
||

Stockists

UK and Europe
For crepe paper and floristry supplies
Floristry Warehouse:
https://floristrywarehouse.com
Arlo Arts:
https://.arloarts.co.uk
Cowling and Wilcox:
https://www.cowlingandwilcox.com
Cartotenica Rossi in Italy:
https://www.cartotecnicarossi.it/
Etsy
https://www.etsy.com

For sundries and wire
eBay or florist supply stores

US
Carte Fini
https://www.cartefini.com
Crepe Paper Store
https://crepepaperstore.com/

Acknowledgments

Thank you to everyone who has helped make this book possible.

To Jon. I don't know what I would do without you. Thank you for all the sacrifices you've made yourself to support me and for your never-ending patience and understanding. I'm so lucky to have you by my side.

To Sophie Allen and Pavilion Books for giving me this amazing opportunity, I'm so incredibly grateful. Thank you for your guidance and being so wonderful to work with. Thank you to Sarah Prior and Anne Sheasby for all your help with editing and proofreading.

To the creative team who brought such beauty to this book and have inspired me so much. Thank you to Alice Kennedy-Owen for wonderful design and styling. To Ola O. Smit for your beautiful photography and patience in working through every tutorial step with me. Thank you as well to Milly Bruce for such gorgeous styling and props.

To Grace Bonney and Design*Sponge for bringing so much attention to my work in the early days as well as to the craft of paper flower making. You are so incredibly generous and I'm very grateful.

Thank you to Brittany Jepson of House that Lars Built for teaching me to make my very first paper flowers. What an inspiration you are.

Thank you to those who have given me support and guidance on my work and making a book: Adeline Klam, Eriko Kondo, Sandra Goncalves and Emma Block, as well as all those that have attended my workshops and supported me. I have learnt so much from you.

Last but not least, thank you to my darling boy Grayson for always helping me to see what is most important.